KATABASIS

10 St Martin's Close, London NW1 0HR
Telephone and Fax: 020 7485 3830
Email: katabasis@katabasis.co.uk
Website : http://www.katabasis.co.uk

Saturday, 16 December 2000

Katabasis is pleased to send you for review its new title:

The Poetry of Earth

by

Dinah Livingstone

Price: £8.95

Katabasis would be grateful to receive a copy of any review you publish.

Trade Distribution: Central Books, 99 Wallis Road, London E9 5LN (020 8986 4854)

THE POETRY OF EARTH

By Dinah Livingstone

Poetry Pamphlets:
Beginning (1967)
Tohu Bohu (1968)
Maranatha (1969)
Ultrasound (1974)
Prepositions and Conjunctions (1977)
Love in Time (1982)
Glad Rags (1983)
Something Understood (1985)
St Pancras Wells (1991)
Poetry Books:
Saving Grace (1987)
Keeping Heart (1989)
Second Sight (1993)
May Day (1997)
Time on Earth: Selected and New Poems (1999)
Edited:
Camden Voices Anthology 1978-1990 (1990)
Work: An Anthology (1999)
Prose:
Poetry Handbook for Readers and Writers (1992)
The Poetry of Earth (2000)

HER TRANSLATIONS INCLUDE:
Poetry:
Poems, Lorca and John of the Cross; *Nicaraguan Mass (Misa campesina)*, Carlos Mejía Godoy; *Nicaraguan New Time*, Ernesto Cardenal; *Anthology of Latin American Poets in London*, (part:); *Dawn Hunters and other Poems*, Roberto Rivera-Reyes (part); *The Nicaraguan Epic*, Carlos & Luis Enrique Mejía Godoy and Julio Valle-Castillo; *The Music of the Spheres*, Ernesto Cardenal; *Prayer in the National Stadium*, María Eugenia Bravo Calderara; *Poets of the Nicaraguan Revolution*; *Life for Each*, Daisy Zamora; *Nosotras: Poems by Nicaraguan Women*,
Prose:
Nature and Grace, Karl Rahner; *In the Kingdom of Mescal*, Georg Schäfer; *The Truth is Concrete*, Dorothee Sölle; *The Poor Sinner's Gospel*, Wilhelm Weitling; *The Tupamaros*, Alain Labrousse; *The Desert is Fertile*, Helder Camara; *Love*, Ernesto Cardenal; *Simplicity*, G. Lefebvre; *This Day is Ours*, J. Leclercq; *The Liturgy*, J. Gelineau; *Jesús de Gramoven*, A. Pérez Esclarín; *We are like Dreamers*, Walter Beyerlin; *The Crucified Peoples*, Jon Sobrino; *Death and Life in Morazán*, M. López Vigil; *The Future of Liberation Theology. Essays in Honour of Gustavo Gutiérrez* (part:); *Companions of Jesus: The Murder and Martyrdom of the Salvadorean Jesuits*, Jon Sobrino; *Moses*, Luis Alonso Schökel; *Mysterium Liberationis: A Dictionary of Liberation Theology*, ed. Ignacio Ellacuría & Jon Sobrino (part); *Our Cry for Life: A Feminist View of Liberation Theology*, María Pilar Aquino; *Santo Domingo and After*, Gustavo Gutiérrez, Jon Sobrino and others (part); *Carlos, Now the Dawn's No Fond Illusion*, Tomás Borge; *Angels of Grace*, Anselm Grün; *We Will Not Dance on our Grandparents' Tombs: Indigenous Uprisings in Ecuador*, Kintto Lucas; *Zapatista Stories*, Subcomandante Marcos

THE
POETRY OF EARTH

Dinah Livingstone

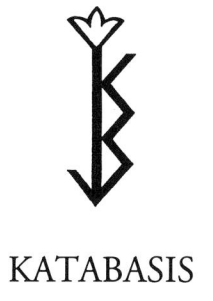

KATABASIS

First published in 2000 by KATABASIS
10 St Martins Close, London NW1 0HR (020 7485 3830)
Email: katabasis@katabasis.co.uk
Website: http://www.katabasis.co.uk

Copyright © Dinah Livingstone 2000
Printed and bound by SRP, Exeter (01392 211909)
The front cover painting is by Anna Mieke Lumsden
Typeset in-house mainly in 12 point Garamond

Trade Distribution: Central Books
99 Wallis Road
London E9 5LN
(020 8986 4854)

ISBN: ISBN 0904872 34 3

British Library Cataloguing in Publication Data:
A catalogue record for this book is available
from the British Library.

CONTENTS

INTRODUCTION 1

CHAPTER I Home on Earth 4

CHAPTER II Word on Earth 26

CHAPTER III Time on Earth 50

CHAPTER IV Down to Earth 76
    1 The Poetic Genius and the Spirit of Prophecy 76
    2 The Human Form Divine 107

CHAPTER V More Things in Heaven and Earth 135
    1 The Deep Power of Joy 138
    2 Self Flashes off Frame and Face 158

CHAPTER VI Mortal Beauty 179

ACKNOWLEDGMENTS

Parts of this book in earlier versions have appeared in *Acumen, Agenda, Sea of Faith* and *The Ethical Record*. The chapter 'Home on Earth' was first given as a talk at the South Place Ethical Society.

I would like to thank my proof readers Kelly Walker and Grace Livingstone and all those who read chapters of the book in draft and made useful comments.

Acknowledgments are due to Hearing Eye and Menard Press for permission to reprint the poem 'Place' from A.C. Jacobs, *Collected Poems and Selected Translations* (Hearing Eye/Menard Press, London 1996).

On the Grasshopper and the Cricket

The poetry of Earth is never dead;
When all the birds are faint with the hot sun,
And hide in cooling trees, a voice will run
From hedge to hedge about the new-mown mead;
That is the Grasshopper's — he takes the lead
In summer luxury — he has never done
With his delights; for when tired out with fun
He rests at ease beneath some pleasant weed.
The poetry of Earth is ceasing never:
On a lone winter evening, when the frost
Has wrought a silence, from the stove there shrills
The Cricket's song, in warmth increasing ever,
And seems to one in drowsiness half lost,
The Grasshopper's among some grassy hills.

John Keats

INTRODUCTION

This is not a specialist work but a common essay, whose argument covers poetry, ecology, theology and politics, which means that the book goes against the trend towards 'niche-marketing'. Extracts in earlier versions have appeared in *Acumen, Agenda, Sea of Faith, The Ethical Record* (after a talk at the South Place Ethical Society), and in the Common Words anthology *Home*. The positive response these received encouraged me to finish and publish the whole.

What Keats called 'the poetry of Earth' is the abundance and diversity of the natural world — the grasshopper in summer, the cricket in winter and so on. This essay broadens the definition to include both the natural world and the abundance and diversity of human cultures and languages, which are at present threatened by aggressive market forces that commodify anything potentially profitable. The definition also includes the poetry – in the usual sense — written in these many languages. Like Blake, it regards religions, for better for worse, as 'creations of the Poetic Genius'.

The book's scope is global and each chapter gives examples, but for practical reasons, the examples have often had to be more local to the author's own culture than the scope of the argument. When I give examples of 'other' cultures, these are often from Latin America, which I have learnt about partly through translating Latin American work, both poetry and prose, over many years. However, the book concerns the whole Earth and in acknowledging this limitation, I invite readers to enjoy themselves brooding on many possible more far-flung examples of their own.

Chapter I, *Home on Earth*, looks at the abundance, diversity and particularity of human cultures and natural species. Chapter II,

Word on Earth, looks at languages. Chapter III, *Time on Earth,* looks at poetries arising out of different traditions. It discusses poetry and presence and how the poem's present moment can hold a whole past history and look forward to the future 'all at once'. Part 1 of chapter IV, *Down to Earth,* discusses religions as creations of the Poetic Genius and how they have been used for repression and liberation. Part 2 is a 'theological recapitulation' on 'The Human Form Divine'. It looks at the Christian theology of Incarnation and Trinity and considers what insights these offer us about humanity and poetry.

The essay is full of quotations, from among which certain key quotations are purposely repeated in different chapters, to illuminate different contexts and hold the book together. In particular, chapter IV, *Down to Earth* returns in the context of religions to certain quotations that have occurred in the previous three chapters, particularly chapter I on natural and cultural diversity.

Chapter V, *More Things in Heaven and Earth,* is also divided into two parts. Part 1, 'The Deep Power of Joy', discusses what 'mystical' poetry might mean to atheists. Starting from Eckhardt's concept of 'isness', it takes three English and one Spanish poet as its main examples: Wordsworth, Coleridge, Hopkins and John of the Cross. Part 2, 'Self Flashes off Frame and Face', begins with Hopkins' favourite philosopher, Duns Scotus' concept of 'thisness' and relates it to the self, both of non-human and human beings. It finishes by looking at the 'thisness' of a poem.

By way of conclusion, the short chapter VI, *Mortal Beauty,* summarises the qualities the essay has discussed as belonging to the poetry of Earth, both what we create and what perceive. The chapter also recapitulates the essay's argument that, through commodification, capitalism threatens the poetry of Earth by attacking both the environment and human lives. Although it is not for poetry to dictate the political tactics to oppose these destructive forces, poetic beauty, in Hopkins' words:

> ... does this: keeps warm
> Men's wits to the things that are; what good means...

In his sonnet Keats said, 'The poetry of Earth is never dead.' The Earth and humanity have marvellous powers of renewal, but our present system is horrendously wasteful both of the Earth and of human lives, and we must find a way of looking after them better.

CHAPTER I
HOME ON EARTH

> For the Earth with all her Fruits of Corn, Cattle, and such like, was made to be a common Storehouse of Livelihood to all Mankind, friend and foe, without exception.
> GERRARD WINSTANLEY, *A Declaration from the Poor Oppressed People of England* (1649).

I live in Camden Town. Over the last few years Camden Town Station has become more and more unpleasant, especially at weekends when it is crammed with tourists going to Camden Market. I feel alien and tense as I make my way through the crowds. Five minutes later, I cut through St Martin's Gardens, where familiar children are playing on the roundabout and swings or kicking a ball. I turn into my street where neighbours call out greetings, go through my front door, upstairs, put the kettle on and sink down on the sofa with Dapple, my cat, beside me. I am at home. London is like that. One moment you feel you are in the Great Wen and a few moments later you are in a sort of village, then snug at home.

So what does home mean? As human beings, we live in relationships of varying degrees of intimacy and we use the word 'home' to refer to the spaces appropriate to these. At its most intimate, home is the household, a place we need as a secure shelter to sleep, eat, perhaps mate, produce and bring up children. Home is the space — room, flat, house, igloo etc. — where we dwell, by ourselves or in a small group, and nurture ourselves and each other. People may like to think of this home as their 'castle', where they can shut the door on 'the world'. Perhaps it meets a need for solitude, privacy and withdrawal as well as being a space for intimate or family relationships. Home is indoors. Home is a place for myself, where I can be by myself, be myself. Home is a place that belongs to me, a place where I belong. Home is a place of my own, where I can be on my own or be with my own. (The word 'own' is related to 'owe' — so in this sense, 'a place of my own' is what is 'owen' i.e. owed to me, as a human being.) Speaking of a wider community, people may speak of 'my home town' or of their 'island home'. Societies or communities in which people feel at home or homeless vary in size from the hamlet to the so-called global village. Most people belong to more than one. Finally, the Earth itself, with all its creatures not just human beings, is our home.

In England, there are many different kinds of households, which people make their home. The number of one-person households is increasing fast, homes where single people live by themselves, on their own, a state in which they may take pleasure or feel very unhappy. If they are happy, they will say they feel 'at home'; others have simply despaired of finding a partner. On the other hand, there are communes, where quite large numbers of people who are not all kin make a home together. Conventionally, home is the 'service station' of the family, a couple with about two children, an intimate group, giving each other many pains and pleasures, living together in the 'family home' (provided, of course, that they have one). Although much violence and many murders in our society are domestic, both conventional and unconventional homes are would-be havens. Frequently, home and family provide some of life's greatest enjoyments.

Within the options available to them, people try to create an immediate environment, in which they and their family can be nurtured, be comfortable, rest and grow. Given the choice, some prefer the town and others the country. Some Londoners find the country intensely tedious or claim they 'couldn't sleep a wink' because they were disturbed by animal noises in the early morning, whereas they can sleep 'like a log' through traffic. On the other hand, I have heard country people say, 'They folks be mad in London. Always rushing about!' Of course the pastoral idyll — thatched cottage with roses round the door — which has had such a firm grip on the English romantic imagination for centuries, is usually far from the reality.

However, in our society, 'a home to call your own' is not regarded as 'owen' (or owed) to everyone. Homes are commodities to be bought and sold. One property company (such as the Church of England) can own (but certainly not in the sense of being 'owen' or owed) thousands of houses. At the same time, many people are homeless. In the Thatcher years we began to see the annual increase of homeless beggars in the streets of London going hand in hand with the encouragement of 'home ownership' in a predatory market, where many of these homes were quickly repossessed and the hapless mortgagees evicted. If we believe a home is own, that is 'owen' or owed to every human being or family, then society needs to work out forms of 'tenure' in which everyone can have a home of their own, with no one excluded. This home-ownership, which is essential to human well-being (just as foxes have holes and the birds of the air have their nests), appears to be incompatible with huge companies trading for profit in property or individuals acquiring titles to too much of it. A few years ago many people found it repugnant to trade in water. Will air be next?

Even within one society, England, different people make their homes in different ways and do not all conform to the standard family image. This variety and individuality enriches the society. At the most basic level, individual eccentricities and 'goings-on' provide entertainment and gossip in a small village or street (though it is always possible for things to turn nasty). Human beings are extremely adaptable and can thrive in many different environments. Throughout the world, there are many different societies, whose ideas of home may differ.

Far north in the arctic regions of Russia, on the Chukotka peninsula, the Chukchi people have lived since prehistoric times. An article in *The Guardian*[1] describes the life of Uikhtikak, a young reindeer herder, who has recently returned from boarding school in Konergino, a village half an hour away by helicopter, to live with his family in the tundra in two conical deerskin tents. Uikhtikak told the *Guardian* journalist, 'We live fine. The herd's in its place. It's not hard to live if you learn well. Why did I come here? It's my character. Everyone's different.' However, the older Chukchis who cherish their traditions also want to preserve the best aspects of the old Soviet system. Vere Girgina, a folk singer in Konergino said, 'We need to find a middle way, so as not to forget the ways of our ancestors, but not to abandon the things we've learned in Soviet times.'

Across the world in Nigeria, approximately half a million Ogoni[2] people live in the Rivers State Region. This is an area of 650 square km — giving a high population density. The Niger delta is a very fertile area and traditionally the Ogoni have made a good living from farming and fishing. In 1958, when Nigeria was still a British colony, the British-Dutch company Shell began extracting oil from this region and continues to do so in partnership with the Nigerian government. Not only did the Ogoni people get nothing for the mineral rights to their lands, but the agricultural land was devastated by flares, spills, blowouts and overground pipelines constructed at a far lower safety standard than would be tolerated in the First World. As an Ogoni song expresses it:

---

[1] 14th December 1998.
[2] Some websites: http://www.gem.co.za/ELA/
http://www.wadham.ox.ac.uk/~rhouston/action/shell_leaflet.html
See also: *Ogoni's Agonies,* edited by Abdul Rasheed Na'Allah (Africa World Press Inc, Trenton, USA 1998).

'Flames of Shell are flames of Hell.' Shell has extracted around $2 billion worth of oil from the Ogoni region and profits from this oil provide 90% of the foreign-owned income to prop up the Nigerian military dictatorship. The Ogoni have received nothing. 20,000 have been displaced from their homes, over 1,500 killed and 30 villages burned to the ground; for the rest, pollution has destroyed their livelihood. For protesting against this crime, as is well known, the military government executed Ken Saro-Wiwa and eight other activists on Friday 10th November 1995.

Known as the Mauberes, the people of East Timor[3] consist of at least twelve ethnic groups, each of which has its own language. Of these, the Tetum language became a lingua franca under Portuguese colonial rule. The East Timorese were mostly farmers, living in isolated mountain areas and attached to their lands by animistic practices. For example, stones, animals, wells and streams were endowed with magical powers, beneficent or malignant, and were known as *lulik*, meaning sacred and intangible. As well as a female fertility god, they invoked a male fertility god, whose name was Bahú-Mau.

After its Carnation Revolution of 1974, Portugal withdrew from its colonies. East Timor enjoyed a brief period of independence but was then invaded on 7th December 1975 by its powerful neighbour, Indonesia. More than 200,000 Timorese were killed in this invasion, which took place hours after the visit of US President Ford and Secretary of State Kissinger to the Indonesian dictator, Suharto. The horrendous human rights violations committed by Indonesia against the Timorese people have been well documented.

---

[3] Websites giving information about East Timor are:
http://www.easttimor.org/
http://www.etan.org

As well as mass killings, torture and other crimes, Indonesia removed an estimated 80% of the Timorese population from their homes and lands, to which they had such a strong religious attachment. They were either put into camps or resettled far from home in towns with no land from which to survive, or in new 'guided villages', where they had to adapt to new crops and farming techniques, not to mention the prevalence of malaria.

Indonesia pursued a vigorous policy of 'Indonesianisation', whose intention was completely to annihilate Timorese social and culture structures and practices. The Timorese were forced to learn a foreign national anthem and state creed ('Pancasila') and indoctrinated with ideas of Indonesian nationhood and the responsibilities of 'new Indonesian man'. The Indonesian military commander of East Timor complained that although his forces were doing their best to bring 'the new Indonesian civilisation to Timor' it was not easy 'to civilise these backward people'.

Of course, Indonesia was interested in East Timor's resources, taking control, for example of the territory's most profitable commodity export, coffee. Although the Indonesian invasion of East Timor was condemned by the UN, Western governments and capitalist companies accepted the *de facto* Indonesian possession of East Timor, despite all the human right abuses. In the 1970's and 1980's Indonesia was important to the US as the main regional anti-communist force in the Cold War. Australia's main concern has been to secure a large share of the oil in the Timor Gap. The Timor Gap oilfield is one of the richest in the world and if East Timor became independent, it would come within East Timor's territorial waters, rather than Indonesia's and Australia's. Western countries (Britain, in particular) are keen to sell sophisticated expensive weaponry to Indonesia and for companies relocating or outsourcing to Indonesia, labour costs are very low.

In 1999 Indonesia and Portugal signed a UN-brokered agreement for an election on the future of East Timor. Despite massive intimidation from the Indonesian government, 98.6% of those registered to vote went to the polls on August 30th 1999. On September 4th 1999, the UN announced that 78.5% of the East Timorese had voted for independence. The Indonesian government retaliated by killing an estimated 1,500 people, displacing a further 100,000 into refugee camps after destroying their homes. East Timor is now ruled by a UN transitional administration (UNATAET) with independence expected within two to three years. Though this is a victory for the brave people of East Timor, it will take a lot more than independence for them really to get back home.

No one knows how long Aboriginal people have lived in Australia, but it may have been at least 40,000 years. They believe that life began during a mythological period known as the 'Dreaming', during which the world was formed by spirit beings. 'They moved across the land, creating the shape of the territory as they went and thus leaving signs of their spiritual presence. Many physical features of the landscape were thought to be formed by these beings, and the sites are consequently held to be sacred.'[4] As one Nyungar Aborigine, Ken Colbung, put it:

> I am sure that people who are not of aboriginal descent are unaware of the strong emotional feeling we have for a particular place. We see it as part of our spiritual background; and that is what is being consistently undermined. The problem is not simply one of mining and the royalties which, at least in part, should come to us. It is one of *land.*'

---

[4] David Crystal, *The Cambridge Encyclopaedia of Language* (Cambridge University Press, 1997), from which the Ken Colbung quotation is also taken.

In many parts of the world traditional forms of agriculture have been supplanted by agribusiness, but it was reported that when Hurricane Mitch hit Honduras, the areas which were farmed in the traditional indigenous way, planting seeds in a hole poked with a stick, suffered less damage than areas where agribusiness had cleared huge areas and made the soil on hillsides much more unstable. This was in addition to the part played by global warming — to which industrial pollution has contributed — in causing the Hurricane in the first place.

About 20,000 of the Huichol people remain in the remote Sierra Madre mountains of Mexico. Formerly, they were free to roam and hunt through a vast territory but now they live off the crops — mainly maize — which they can grow in their difficult upland soil. Now even here they are threatened by logging and environmental damage. They are famous for their beautiful embroidery in brilliant colours and still maintain their ancient, pre-Aztec shamanic cult, including a yearly cycle of pilgrimages.

One pilgrimage is to the sea, the source of life. Another is to Viricota (which means Valley of Flowers) their mythical place of origin where Tamatz Kallaumari, the blue deer god comes to Earth. In his footprints the peyote cactus sprouted, producing the mescalin which gives shaman and people their sacred visions. Maize, peyote and the deer are all gods and form a trinity:

> The blue flower, the beautiful flowers
> of Viricota have become
> the feathered wands of Tataveri.
> They are sacred flowers.
> They are the songs of peyote.
> They are memories of Viricota
> sung by the gods of Viricota.[5]

---

5   'Eight Huichol Shaman Poems', translated by Edward Kissam and Michael Schmidt in *Flower and Song* (Anvil Press, London 1977).

In a recent documentary film about the Huichol, their spokesman insisted they performed these rituals in order to look after the Earth, not just for themselves but for everybody. Not all peoples are expansionist and want to dominate or exterminate other peoples with other ways. They just want to be free to live in their own way, with their own religion, which is a strategy for survival, embracing a broader view than capitalism, in its great concern to take care of our mother, the Earth.

The Yanomami people of the Amazon are being destroyed by the invasion of 40,000 goldminers who are poisoning their water courses and spreading diseases against which they have no resistance. In his 'Declaration to all the Peoples of the Earth' Davi Kopenawa Yanomami says:[6]

> All they know about is dealing in money. Our thinking is land. Our interest is to preserve the land in order not to create diseases for the people of Brazil, not just the Indians. We Yanomami are dying because of diseases: malaria, influenza, dysentery... and other diseases which the Indians didn't know, brought by the goldminers from outside.

The indigenous people of Ecuador have one of the best organised movements on the continent. On January 21st 2000, they and their supporters rose up against the proposed dollarisation of the economy and took over the Parliament building in the capital, Quito, to install a 'poncho utopia'. Although the uprising was rapidly defeated, these indigenous peoples continue their struggle for their home and their cultural identity.

---

[6] Boa Vista, Roraima, 28th August 1989, duplicated. Quoted in *Concilium* 1990/6, page 82.

Ecuador is one of the countries with the greatest biodiversity on the planet. Large biomedical companies *steal* plants and then patent some of their medicinal properties, which indigenous peoples have often known about for centuries. It seems that the attempt to patent the whole human genome has been stalled, at least for the time being, but numerous companies are still rushing to patent genetic knowledge for commercial use. Recently, many samples of Ecuadorian indigenous blood were stolen (apparently, by members of US Pentecostal sects) to put on sale in US Genome Boutiques and on the internet. As the indigenous leader, Ricardo Ulcuango says: 'We knew about the stealing of sacred animals and plants like *ayahuasca* but it had not yet reached the point of actually carrying off our brothers' and sisters' blood.'[7] How can human beings feel at home on earth when not only their home and environment are threatened but even their ownership of their own bodies?

The Zapatista uprising on New Year's Day 1994 was against NAFTA,[8] the North American Free Trade Agreement, which benefits big business and makes survival for many poor Mexicans almost impossible. The Zapatista rebels consist mainly of Mayan peasants and although the Chiapas region of Mexico is extremely rich in natural resources, these Mayan peasants are now among the poorest of the poor. They have a slogan: *Por un mundo donde quepan muchos mundos:* 'For a world where there is room for many worlds.' They mean that their way of looking at the world, their world, is different from that of the dominant culture in their country, but they claim the right to be at home in the world in their own way, or as they put it, with their own dignity. In the state of Chiapas, there are about 300,000 indigenous Tzotziles,

---

[7] Quoted in Kintto Lucas, *We will not Dance on our Grandparents' Tombs. Indigenous Uprisings in Ecuador* (CIIR, London 2000).

[8] Recently, the Tory leader, William Hague, made the extraordinary proposal that Britain should join NAFTA, which would certainly bring the Mexican experience closer to home.

120,000 Choles, 90,000 Zoques and 70,000 Tojolabales. These are the original inhabitants of the region, who lived there before the Spaniards came in the fifteenth century. They have their traditional ways, including a tradition of communal farming with a form of land tenure known in Spanish as the *ejido*, and a traditional form of democracy in which all important decisions are discussed by the whole community, until consensus is reached — which has been translated into Spanish as *mandar obedeciendo*, meaning leaders must obey the wishes of those they lead.

In one of his communiqués[9] the Zapatista leader, sub-comandante Marcos, describes how these indigenous Mayans recently built a meeting place for 10,000 people, which turned out to be a giant spiral that could only be fully seen from the air (like other ancient indigenous buildings).

> I want to tell you about an architectural work, which was built at the edge of Guadalupe Tepeyac, when it was still a living village, in July and August 1994. The Tojolabal architects were mostly illiterate with the most 'educated' among them having reached the 3rd grade in primary school. But in 28 days they constructed a building capable of containing ten thousand visitors to what the Zapatistas called the 'National Democratic Convention'. In honour of Mexican history the Zapatistas called the meeting place Aguascalientes. The gigantic meeting place contained an auditorium with seating for ten thousand participants, a platform for one hundred, a library, a computer room,

---

[9] Communiqué from Marcos, dated 23rd October 1996, containing this report by Don Durito de la Lacandona (one of Marcos' characters, who is the Don Quixote of the Lacandona jungle — and a beetle), with comments by Marcos. This communiqué can be found in Spanish on: http://www.sitio.web.com/sitio/index.html
The main Zapatista web address is: http://www.ezln.org/

kitchens, lodging houses, parking. It even had, they said, a 'crime area'.

Faced with the problem of building lodgings, the library and other installations, the indigenous Tojolabal chiefs in the Zapatista insurrection, who now had to improvise as architects, began to build houses in an apparently higgledy-piggledy way. At the time El Sup[10] thought they were merely dotted around the giant auditorium. It was not until he was counting the lodging capacity of each house, that he realised one of the houses was 'crooked'. It had a peculiar sort of break in one of its outside edges. He paid it no more attention.

It was comandante Tacho, a Tojolabal, who asked him:
'What do you think of the spiral?'
'What spiral?'
'The one round the auditorium, of course,' replied comandante Tacho, as if saying, 'There's light in the daytime.'

El Sup stared at him and Tacho realised that El Sup had not understood what he meant. So he took him to the 'crooked' house and showed him the roof where the crossbeams broke off unexpectedly.
'This is where the spiral curves,' said Tacho.

Well. There was the Mayan spiral. The spiral without beginning or end. Where does a spiral begin and where does it end? At its inner limit or its outer limit? Does a spiral go inwards or outwards? The rebel Mayan chiefs' spiral began and ended in the 'safe house' but it also ended in the library, the place for meeting and seeking.

---

10 Durito refers to Marcos as 'El Sup', familiar for *el Subcomandante*: the Subcomandante.

Marcos goes on to say:

> On February 10th 1995, Federal Army air transport troops took Guadalupe Tepeyac. When the Government Army entered Aguascalientes, the first thing it did was to destroy the library and the safe house, the beginning and end of the spiral. Then it set about destroying the rest. For some strange reason, the break-point in the 'crooked' house remained standing for a few months afterwards. According to the story, it only fell down when in December of that year 1995, other Aguascalientes arose in the mountains of South East Mexico.

People living in their traditional way do not necessarily want to reject all the conveniences that modern technology has to offer, but they want to be free to decide for themselves how they will incorporate it into their way of life. They want to call their lives their own and control the technology, not be controlled by it. Famously, the Zapatistas make excellent use of the internet in what has been called a cyber war of information and ideas.

It is interesting to see how the Mayans have modified their own customs to suit demands of the current struggle, for example, against tradition, the Zapatistas have many women leaders, including comandantes Ramona, Trini, Leticia, Hortensia and María Alicia. On the other hand, with the formation of the Zapatista movement, traditional Latin American guerrilla tactics (for example, the guerrilla *foco* or stronghold of an armed 'vanguard' with a hierarchical military command structure demanding implicit obedience) have been modified by Mayan customs of popular democracy.

Human beings make their home in the world in many different ways. They create cultures which are adapted to different climates and suit their own human particularities. This particularity is what the medieval philosopher Duns Scotus called 'thisness' or in Latin *haecceitas*. Thisness, abundance and diversity are the qualities of human life at home on Earth. This life is for its own sake, so we may add a fourth quality and call it 'gratuitousness'. These are the qualities of what Keats called 'the poetry of Earth'.

The neoliberal New World Order — the current aggressive form of global capitalism — threatens these qualities. It threatens the particularity and diversity of cultures, whereas as we saw, the Zapatistas are fighting not just for themselves but for the whole diversity of cultures: *por un mundo donde quepan muchos mundos:* for a world where there is room for many worlds. Capitalism threatens life's abundance for the majority of human beings at home on Earth and it is mortally opposed to life for its own sake. The criterion for the capitalist is the market and profit, to which people's lives are wholly subjected. The market is an idol demanding daily human sacrifice.

As Marcos says in a communiqué, of July 1998:[11]

> Certainly neoliberalism has created a formidable enemy force in large-scale financial capital, an enemy force that can dictate wars, crashes, dictatorships, so-called 'democracies', lives and above all deaths in every corner of the world. Nevertheless, this process of total globalisation (economic, political and cultural) does not mean the inclusion of different societies, incorporating their particularities. On the contrary, it implies the imposition of one single way of thinking: that of financial capital. In this war of conquest everything and all of us are subjected to the criterion of the market — anything that opposes it or presents an obstacle will be eliminated. It implies the

---

[11] Subcomandante Marcos' full communiqué can be found (in Spanish) on: http://www.ezln.org/archive/ezln980717.html

destruction of humanity as a sociocultural collective and reconstructs it as a market place. Opposing neoliberalism, fighting against it, is not just one political or ideological option, it is a question of the survival of humanity.

These are just a few examples but there are countless others and, as we saw at the beginning, the daily human sacrifices demanded by capitalism are not confined to ethnic cultures or the Third World. There are homeless beggars in every Western city, including London.

Human beings share their home on Earth with many other species. The word 'ecology' comes from the Greek word *oikos*, meaning a household. At the beginning we considered the 'household' as the most common meaning of the word 'home'. But our home on Earth, together with all its other creatures, is also a household, belonging to us all and to which we all belong. As Gerrard Winstanley put it, the Earth is our Common Treasury.

Many people enjoy watching nature programmes on television. We are shown the particularities of vast numbers of species and how they depend on each other in a web of life. Not only human cultures, but all life at home on Earth shares the qualities of particularity, diversity, abundance and gratuitousness. Species are mutually dependent on each other in a marvellous 'balance of nature'. We need each other, we provide for each other's needs, we eat each other. There are some languages in which the word for 'love' is the same as the word for 'eat'.

Here are some examples from David Attenborough's BBC nature books.[12] Some plants actually encourage animals to feed on them. They need to have genetic material, pollen, transported from one

---

[12] For example: *Life on Earth; The Trials of Life; The Life of Birds* (all BBC, London).

individual plant to another. To advertise the fact, they surround the pollen and the anthers that produce it with the vivid petals of a flower. The bumble bee has developed a complex machinery for collecting pollen. The hairs on its furry body are covered with microscopic hooks, which pick up the slightly sticky pollen grains, as the bee busies around the flower. When it flies off, it starts to tidy itself up, sweeping its fur clean with a bristly comb that fringes the lower half of each hind leg.

Of course, most animals do not like to be hunted for food and develop what defences they can. On the open plains of East Africa, grass-eaters — zebra, antelope and gazelle — manage to find protection among their own number. A gazelle, grazing by itself is an easy target for a cheetah. If the gazelle is to feed at all, it has to lower its head, so losing sight of its surroundings. But if the gazelle grazes in a herd of a hundred or so, its chances of survival are dramatically better. It is more likely to get an early warning of the cheetah's approach, for even when its own head is down grazing, other heads are up and scanning the surrounding country. In order to survive, the cheetah must catch some prey, but it will catch what it needs to eat and it will not exterminate a whole herd. The balance of nature is maintained.

Some creatures live on each other literally. Many of the big animals of Africa — eland and buffalo, warthog and rhino — are attended by oxpeckers, birds that belong to the starling family. A giraffe may have a flock of several dozens of them as its regular attendants. They scuttle over its body picking off fleas and ticks and maggots, clambering into its ears, probing beneath its tail. They are so at home on the giraffe's body that they perform their courtship displays there. The birds provide a very real service, so the large animals allow them freedom to wander into the clefts and crannies of their bodies. In return for this valet service, the birds get blood from the ticks and also some from any small cuts in the large animals themselves.

Animals make all kinds of homes on Earth. To create a home they become potters and plasterers, weavers and needleworkers, miners, masons, scaffolders, thatchers and sculptors. The oven bird of Paraguay spends months each year constructing a roofed chamber very like the traditional ovens used by people in those parts. For the tailor bird of India its beak is a needle. As thread it uses spiders' silk, cotton from seeds and fibres from bark. It selects leaves that are still attached to the tree and pulls them into position so that their edges overlap. Then it pierces a hole in the margins and threads the fibre through it. It twists the end of the stitch into a knot. The South American oropendola and several other species actually weave their nests. Bower birds decorate their bowers to attract females. For example the Vogelkop gardener of New Guinea may decorate its bower with black beetle wing covers, scarlet berries, shiny black fruits, huge squat acorns of the local oak, fragments of orange fungi and a great heap of orange coloured dead leaves. Many religions praise God for his creation. Those who do not praise the Lord still praise the wonders of life on Earth *for themselves.*

Just as capitalism threatens the particularity, diversity and abundance of human life at home on Earth, and will not allow that life to be for its own sake, so it threatens all other creatures at home on Earth who are not profitable to it. Species extinction is a natural part of the evolutionary process. The World Conservation Monitoring Centre in Cambridge reports that in the last 400 years 641 species have become extinct. However, due to human activities, species and ecosystems are more threatened today than ever before in recorded history. In particular, the losses are taking place in tropical forests, where over 90 per cent of identified species live. In 1996 there were 5,205 species, including 1,096 species of mammals on the endangered list. It is estimated that, at the present rate, two to eight percent of the Earth's species will disappear over the next 25 years. The

Secretariat for the Convention on Biological Diversity reports:[13] 'Based on current trends, an estimated 34,000 plant and 5,200 animal species face extinction.'

Here are just two more examples. The Great Barrier Reef is dying.[14] A combination of trawling, the chemical run-off from land clearing, oil-shale mining, and the effects of coral bleaching caused by global warming is killing the reef. The reef is one of the world's richest natural sites, which is home to more than 400 species of corals, 1,500 fish species, 4,000 kinds of molluscs and 260 species of birds... The scientists' report reveals that large-scale prawn trawling — both illegal and licensed — has in a few years reduced sea-bed animals by more than half along the 1,200 mile long coral reef. For every tonne of prawns caught, up to 10 tonnes of marine life is being sacrificed. To return to the example of Shell in Ogoniland: the Niger delta is home to coastal rainforest, mangrove habitats and wetlands. It has been identified by the UN as the most endangered river delta in the world, as a result of four decades of oil exploitation.

The threat to biological diversity is not only an environmental tragedy. It also threatens the livelihood of poor people in many parts of the world, who depend on their local biological resources. It lacks respect for life by exterminating so many species and making the poor even poorer. It also lacks respect for the human species as a whole, as we do not know what harm we may be doing to ourselves in the future by eliminating plants and animals, that could, for example, provide an antidote to some new plague. Growing concern over this unprecedented threat to biodiversity inspired negotiations for a legally binding instrument to reverse the alarming trend. On 5th June 1992 at the Rio Earth

---

[13] The Convention's website is at http://www.biodiv.org. The quotation above is from its 'Guide to the Convention' on this website, which also lists each country's ratification status.

[14] Report in *The Guardian* on January 14th 1999.

Summit, the Convention on Biological Diversity was opened for signature. Its stated aims were 'the conservation of biological diversity, the sustainable use of its components and the fair and equitable sharing of the benefits arising out of the utilisation of genetic resources.' It comes as no surprise that so far the USA has refused to ratify this Convention.

Human beings are part of Earth's ecology, its *oikos*, household. We must treat our household and its members with respect. However, this does not mean that human problems can be solved simply by going 'back to nature'. This has often been an agenda for oppression of the excluded 'other'. A group or class of people may be designated as 'the natural' in a particular society and therefore by a curious logic regarded as inferior and excluded from full participation in the society's benefits. Historically, this has happened to women in many cultures and to the Indian or so-called 'noble savage'. It happens today in many forms of racism or when women are both excluded from the priesthood (the officer/managerial class) and forbidden to use contraception by the Catholic Church.

As we saw with the Chukchi people of the Russian Arctic, the Ogoni of Nigeria and with the Zapatistas, so-called 'ethnic' cultures are not static, any more than Western cultures are. They want to be free to take what they need from the modern world to use in their own way. They also want justice. This is not necessarily provided by the 'balance of nature'. Balance on the human scale is justice, a human creation that has to be struggled for — a going forward, rather than a going back. Human beings cannot just go 'back to nature' because we have language. We are, by nature, linguistic animals, and although we belong to the *oikos*, household, of planet Earth, through language, human beings can create, as the Zapatistas would say, 'many worlds'. As well as in a particular place, we are also at home in our mother tongue. This is the subject of the next chapter.

Wanting justice on Earth and the respect for other cultures that this implies do not mean that we should not subject ideas or practices we find offensive to ethical criticism, just because they are 'ethnic'. It does not mean, for example, that we must agree with female circumcision and infibulation, out of a false reverence for 'cultural diversity'. The same goes for the cultures of the past. They were not perfect just because they were 'indigenous'. As well as struggling to create a future, indigenous or ethnic cultures have a history, in which many forces played a part.

With enormous scholarship, Ernesto Cardenal has written a huge range of poems constituting his *Homage to the American Indians*.[15] Among these, his poem 'Quetzalcóatl' tells the story of the historical/mythical god-king Quetzalcóatl, the 'Plumed Serpent' (also 'Precious Twin') who was born in the year '1-Cane' (843 AD) and ruled the Toltecs in Tula. It is impossible in this brief space to do justice to the rich complexity of this poem, but this is its main story. The Toltecs were a Nahuatl-speaking tribe who ruled throughout central Mexico four centuries before the Aztecs. The Toltecs developed a high culture in art, architecture, poetry and astronomy. Quetzalcóatl, their ruler, forbade human sacrifices and his cult was monotheistic. For refusing to allow human sacrifices, he was thrown out of the city. He went off to Tlapalan and disappeared into the sea, telling his people he would be back. He became Venus the evening star. In the words of Cardenal's poem:

> Venus invisible for 90 days.
> Then it shines for 250 days in the evening sky.
> Then it disappears for eight days
> and reappears in the east as the morning star.

---

[15] Collected in the bilingual text *Golden UFOs*, translated by Carlos and Monique Altschul (Indiana University Press, USA 1992).

(the descent into Hell).
Quetzalcóatl eight days among the dead.

Or as the ancient Aztec poem puts it:[16]

He was not seen for four days, as he had gone
to the realm of the dead — he returned
with arrows in his fist, and after eight days
he became a great star.

After Quetzalcóatl the Aztecs came with their god Huitzilopochtli, the god of sun and war, demanding human sacrifice. Cardenal's poem 'Quetzalcóatl' continues:

They set the turquoise serpent (Huitzilopochitli)
against the quetzal-feathered serpent (Quetzalcóatl).
Now Huitzilopochtli
Lord of war:
supreme god.
After the defeat of Quetzalcóatl's worshippers
human sacrifices.

But there was resistance, the Tlamatinimes, whom Cardenal calls antifascists. They kept alive the teaching of Quetzalcóatl and 'taught children how to live': they must strenuously avoid evil and 'a human being must be honoured like a precious stone and rich plumage'.

Respect for indigenous cultures does not therefore mean regarding everything about them as indiscriminately good, just because it is 'ethnic'. Every culture has its own history and ethical struggles. But respect *does* mean valuing the Earth, our home, our household, *oikos,* and the human and other life on it. It *does* mean

---

[16] Translated in *Flower and Song* (Anvil Press, 1977).

appreciating the distinguishing characteristics of life on Earth — abundance, diversity, particularity and gratuitousness — and allowing them to flourish. As Hopkins puts it in his sonnet 'Inversnaid':

> What would the world be, once bereft
> Of wet and of wildness? Let them be left,
> O let them be left, wildness and wet;
> Long live the weed and the wilderness yet.

Capitalism lacks this respect. It has turned Mammon into an idol, to which all life on Earth, whether plant, animal or human is sacrificed if they stand in its way.

In his lecture *How we Live and How we Might Live*, William Morris said:

> It is not an original remark, but I make it here, that my home is where I meet people with whom I sympathise, whom I love.

Firstly, of course, this applies to our own intimate circle, but then Ellen, the heroine of *News from Nowhere*, expands our sympathies when at the end of the book, she gives her great cry: 'How I love the Earth, and the seasons and weather, and all things that deal with it and all that grows out of it.'

Let them be left, O let them be left! Augustine defined love by saying *Amor meus pondus meum:* 'my love is my weight' — my gravity.[17] Gravity keeps our feet on the ground; love attaches us to the Earth which is our home.

---

[17] Augustine of Hippo, *Confessions,* translated by Henry Chadwick (Oxford World Classics, 1991), page 278.

CHAPTER II
WORD ON EARTH

There are about six thousand languages on Earth, which, like plant and animal species, are related to each other in families or phyla and grow and develop like living organisms. The previous chapter stressed the qualities of abundance, diversity, particularity and gratuitousness as characteristic of life on Earth — of its species and its human cultures. We called this, in Keats' phrase, 'the poetry of Earth'. These four qualities are also shared by the languages spoken on Earth. All these many languages are used for communication by this or that particular human group — for everyday tasks, for debate about what should be done and for stories and poetry. It is appropriate and delightful that language, the instrument we use to create a particular culture (or world, as the Zapatistas would say), should be for each a mother tongue in which to be at home, and should share the four characteristics of life on Earth, that give it both its homeliness and its zest.

To speak a language the human mouth produces a set of sounds — called phonemes — whose distinctions distinguish meaning. Although the human mouth is much the same throughout the species, other languages use different sets of sounds. As well as having different sets of phonemes and different vocabularies, languages have different grammars, with different constructions. Does this mean they construct the world differently? Even within languages, there are many different accents and dialects, which attach people to different places and add to the sense of being at home. Both dialects and languages throughout the world produce poetry, which may be regarded as the 'quintessence' of a language, which voices the 'poetry of Earth'.

This chapter will consider briefly what we mean by a language and some examples of the sounds and grammars of different languages and dialects. It will look in a little more detail at my own mother tongue, the sounds, grammar and prosody of English. It will ask why, when difference of language can be used to support a poisonous nationalism, it matters that so many languages are becoming extinct. Although they operate inseparably, this chapter will focus on what we may call the mechanics of a language, whereas the following chapter, *Time on Earth*, will focus on language as the voice of a cultural tradition.

So what is language? Darwin called it 'an instinctive tendency to acquire an art' and Stephen Pinker develops this idea in his book *The Language Instinct*.[18] He uses the term instinct, because 'it conveys the idea that people know how to talk in more or less the sense that spiders know how to spin webs'. Pinker rejects the behaviourism of Watson and Skinner and follows Chomsky in describing language as a biological adaptation by which we communicate with one another. A preschool child's tacit knowledge of grammar is more sophisticated than the thickest grammar book or the most state-of-the-art computer language and the same applies to all healthy human beings. Because language is an *instinct* belonging to the whole human species, the languages of so-called primitive peoples are no less complex than a modern language like 20th century Mandarin Chinese.

Pinker describes how in 1930 the Australian gold prospector Michael Leahy climbed the mountains of New Guinea and came to a previously unexplored plateau, where he met Stone Age people, who had been isolated from the rest of the world for 4,000 years:

---

[18] Stephen Pinker, *The Language Instinct* (Penguin, 1994).

The women and children gradually got up courage to approach also, and presently the camp was swarming with the lot of them, all running about and jabbering.

The 'jabbering' was language. Throughout history, whenever there are reports of one people encountering another for the first time, all of them already have language, which is no mere jabber but a medium that can express abstract concepts, invisible entities and intricate reasoning. Complex language is universal which, Pinker says, is the first reason to suspect that language is not just a cultural invention but the product of a special human instinct.

In *The Language of Genes*[19] Steve Jones argues that languages behave in a similar way to genes and like genes, they evolve. 'Any entity — be it a language or a pool of genes — which remains isolated from its fellow will begin to evolve away from them. There are parallels between the process of biological evolution and those which produce new languages from a common ancestor.' For example, English is similar though not identical to German for the same reason that foxes are similar though not identical to wolves: English and German are modifications of a common ancestor language spoken in the past, just as foxes and wolves are modifications of a common ancestor species that lived in the past.

Jones goes on to argue that this is more than an analogy because 'Family trees of language look so similar to those based on the sharing of genes as to suggest a common history.' This makes sense if as a general rule people are more likely to marry and have children with a partner who speaks their language. (There are of course exceptions, called 'isolates', such as the Basque language, which may be a leftover language from the time before the Indo-Europeans arrived in the area.) Broadly speaking, languages can

---

[19] Steve Jones, *The Language of Genes* (Flamingo, 1994).

be classified like biological species — some say into just seventeen distinct families or phyla. We can make a tree of the world's languages and when it is put next to the genetic tree, they look intriguingly similar.

English belongs to the Indo-European family, descended from an extinct language called 'Proto-Indo-European'. Scholars dispute where Indo-European originated. One theory is that the Indo-Europeans lived in Anatolia (in modern Turkey) from around 7000 BC. Or they may have been a Stone-Age people known as the Kurgans, living in the steppe region of southern Russia around 4000 BC, whose culture seems to have arrived in the Adriatic region before 2000 BC. They began to spread into the Danube area of Europe around 3500 BC and by 2500 BC they had reached India, Ireland and Scandinavia. Probably, it was the discovery of farming that made them spread so far. Sons and daughters of farmers needed more land and so spread outwards, perhaps intermarrying with the local hunter gatherers.

In the Indo-European family tree there are eight sub-groups, including Germanic, Celtic, Romance, Slavic and Indo-Iranian. These sub-groups have branches. For example, the Indo-Iranian divides into the Iranian branch, from which Persian, Kurdish and other languages descend, and the Indic branch, which has generated Hindi, Urdu, Bengali, Punjabi and other languages spoken in India today.

English belongs to the Western branch of the Germanic sub-group of Indo-European, together with German, Yiddish, Dutch, Flemish and Afrikaans. The Northern branch comprises Swedish, Danish, Norwegian and Icelandic. It is fascinating to see lists of words that are similar in Indo-European languages belonging to the various branches, words such as month, mother, new, night and three.

Like the genetic code in DNA, both the sounds and the grammar of a language are what are called 'discrete combinatorial systems'. These work differently from a 'blending system'. Paint mixing, for example, is a blending system, so that if you mix blue and yellow you get green. A discrete combinatorial system does not 'blend' its elements, which is why it can make 'infinite use of finite media'. In DNA four kinds of nucleotides are combined into sixty-four kinds of codons, which can be strung into an infinite number of different genes.

The sound system of a language is a set of sounds — called phonemes — whose distinctions distinguish meaning. For example, 'pat' and 'bat' mean different things in English, so 'p' and 'b' are phonemes. They are 'minimal pairs', the single phonemic change that alters the word 'pat' to the word 'bat'. In Mandarin Chinese a different tone can make a different word, so the language has 'tonemes'. For example 'ma' can be said with four different tones, which respectively make it mean 'mother', 'hemp', 'horse', 'scold'.

A phonemic system is a discrete combinatorial system that can be combined in an enormous number of ways to form words — with certain restrictions according to the rules of the particular language. Every language has its own particular set or system of phonemes, which differ from and, of course, sometimes overlap with other languages. Every language *sounds* different. That is the material base of the *thisness* of every language. A native English speaker can string together a series of nonsense sounds, and their fellow English speakers will immediately recognise that these sound like French, Russian, German, Italian, as the case may be. The comic possibilities have often been exploited. On the other hand, what is so delightful about the real thing is that Italians really do sound so Italian and Russians so Russian.

In standard English 'r' is a post-alveolar frictionless continuant: 'a red red robin'. In French it is a uvular trill; the French for 'wren' is *le roitelet*. This may even make us feel that a bird called a robin is an English bird and a uvular trilled *roitelet* is a French bird, although of course there are plenty of robins and wrens in both countries.

Sounds which are phonemes in English may not be phonemes in other languages. Eskimo-Aleut has just three vowel phonemes, Spanish has five, and English has twelve (plus eight diphthongs). English has two 'i' sounds: /iː/ as in sheet and /ɪ/ as in shit. To a Spanish speaker these words sound the same. Likewise Italian speakers, whose 'a' sound is a pure cardinal vowel number 4: /a/ as in *alba* (= 'dawn') may not hear the distinction between two sounds, which are phonemes — minimal pairs — in English and formed very near cardinal vowel number 4: the sound /æ/ as in 'ham', which is also a front vowel but slightly closer than /a/ and the sound /ʌ/ as in 'hum', which is a central vowel, formed further back than /a/. So to an Italian who has not learnt to hear the distinction, English 'mud' sounds like 'mad' and 'love' sounds like 'lav'.

Japanese does not distinguish 'r' from 'l'. Professor Pinker relates how when he arrived in Japan shortly after Bill Clinton became US President, the linguist Masaaki Yamanashi greeted him with a twinkle and said: 'We are all very interested in Clinton's erection.'

Other languages use different sounds. For example Xhosa, which has 141 phonemes, uses clicks. There are clicks produced by the lips, tongue tip, tongue body, any of which can be nasalised or not, voiced or not, making as many as 48 different click sounds in all. The reader can try the following three clicks and note how different they sound. An alveolar click (tongue clicks on the gum ridge) is called a 'tut-tut' click. In a lateral or 'gee-up' click, air is released from the side of the tongue. In a retroflex or 'clip-clop' click the tongue is curled backwards. A bilabial click is of course a kiss. Obviously, with these sound systems, languages build very different vocabularies but they also have different grammars, with different constructions.

Grammar has been defined as a set of rules adopted more or less unconsciously by native speakers that produces sentences in a particular language. It is the way native speakers of a language combine their words to convey meaning. Grammar is another discrete combinatorial system, not a blending system. When words are combined in a sentence, you do not get a 'blend' between them but each different combination gives a different meaning. This makes an almost infinite number of possible sentences. Different languages allow different combinations of classes of words, with the word order more or less fixed or free.

According to Chomsky, a visiting Martian scientist would conclude, that aside from their mutually unintelligible vocabularies, earthlings speak a single language. Linguists who follow Chomsky hold that all languages have an underlying Universal Grammar belonging to the human innate 'language instinct'. For example, the vocabulary of all languages is sorted into part-of-speech categories including noun and verb. Universal Grammar is like an archetypal body plan found across vast numbers of animals in a phylum. Although they look so different, all amphibians, reptiles, birds and mammals have a common body architecture with segmented backbone, four jointed limbs, a tail, a skull and so on. But some animals walk on four legs, a bat's wing is a hand, a whale's forelimbs have become flippers.

A strong argument for an innate Universal Grammar is that studies of how children learn to speak show that very early on they can generate grammatical sentences they cannot possibly have heard before, which operate the grammar of the language consistently with the sentences they *have* heard. An infant learns to do this for any language (and sometimes more than one language) that is spoken by the community in which it grows up. However, children are not born speaking any particular language, because each different language has evolved not only its own sounds and vocabulary but its own grammar, that is, its own way of using any Universal Grammar. This particular grammar may classify or sort the world differently, which gives a different 'take' on the world, just as the vocabulary of each language describes the world in words which have their own particular 'feel'.

One large difference is between isolating and inflecting languages. Latin, for example, was an inflecting language. The person, number and tense of a verb is given in the word ending: *amamus* means 'we love' in the present tense; *amabo* means 'I shall love'. Modern Spanish and Italian, both descendants of Latin, also inflect their verbs, which thus acquire about fifty different forms. If verbs are inflected, the pronoun subject can be omitted, so that Spanish *ama* does not have to specify whether the person who is loving is he or she, which can be a useful fudge. Turkish is believed to have two million different verb forms. In Kivunjo, a Bantu language, which is said to make English look like draughts compared with chess, the verb form *Näïkìmlyïïà* meaning 'he is eating it for her' is composed of eight different parts. In Swahili *anayenipatria maji* means 'he who gets water for me'. The verb has eight parts and *maji* means water.[20]

Greek verbs have a Middle voice, between the Active and Passive, which is generally reflexive in meaning. For example, the active is 'I wash' [something], the passive is 'I am washed', the middle is 'I wash' [myself]; the active is 'I stop' [something], the middle is 'I stop [myself] = I cease'. In addition to an intensive, Hebrew has a causative verb form, so that different inflections of

---

[20] This, together with some of the other examples and information in this chapter, is taken from David Crystal, *The Cambridge Encyclopaedia of Language* (Cambridge University Press, 1997).

the same root give: 'suck', 'suck hard', 'suckle'; or 'die', 'die stone dead' and 'kill'. 'To be king or rule' is the simple form whose causative is 'to make king'.

As well as inflecting verbs, Latin inflects nouns into six cases, so that the ending added to the noun tells you whether it is a subject, object or possessive or dative. *Mater amat puellam* means 'the mother loves the girl'; *puellam amat mater* also means 'the mother loves the girl'. Because *puellam* ('girl') is marked with the accusative object marker 'm', the word order of the sentence can be free. In some languages all nouns have gender, masculine and feminine and possibly neuter as well. This is mysterious to English speakers today. For example, in German, the sun, *die Sonne* is feminine and the moon, *der Mond* is masculine. In Romance languages, following Latin, it is the other way round: the sun is masculine (e.g. French: *le soleil*) and the moon is feminine (French: *la lune*). How far do these genders affect the way native speakers look at the world?

Adjectives may also have gender. This can be particularly useful with adjectival nouns. For example, in John of the Cross' love poetry, the two lovers are *Amado* (= beloved, masculine) and *Amada* (= beloved, feminine). The line *Amada en el Amado transformada* is stronger and more graceful than most of its English translations.[21]

Pronouns can be inflected. Though English has a subject, object and possessive form in both singular and plural: I-me-mine; we-us-ours, Latin has twice as many. However, Latin and the languages derived from it are like English in having just a singular and a plural. Recognising the supreme importance of the couple

---

[21] One translation I encountered recently sounds particularly clumsy: 'Mistress transformed into the Lover'. John of the Cross' poetry is discussed further in chapter V, pages 151-7.

or pair, other languages, such as Samoan have a singular: 'I', dual 'we two' and plural 'we' (more than two).

German forms enormous compound words, such as *Weltanschauungsveränderung* meaning 'change in world view', and also relegates the main verb to the end of subordinate clauses, even very long ones, so that you have to wait for it as the key to the whole. Japanese does not have prepositions, it has postpositions, so the word order in Japanese is not 'with me' but 'me with' or 'me you together'.

Even within languages, there are many different dialects and accents — Cockney or Somerset, for example — which attach people to different places and add to the sense of being at home. Yesterday I walked down my street and saw a man with a huge tar barrel. I asked him, 'Are you mending Number Twelve's roof again?' He replied, 'No, Thirteen,' pronounced /fɜːʔiːn/ beginning with an /f/ followed by a long central vowel /ɜː/ and a glorious glottal stop /ʔ/, which made me walk on with a great wave of London pride.

The difference between a language and a dialect has been described by saying a language is a dialect with an army. Dialects not only pronounce the language differently but also have some special words and sometimes different grammar. The Dorset dialect poet William Barnes has a wonderful poem, whose title and refrain are: 'Trees be Company' with its Dorset present tense of the verb 'to be'. Just as it is untrue that so-called 'ethnic' languages are less rich and complex than a dominant modern language, this is also untrue of dialects. Grammar is not a scholarly invention; it is inherent in every language. In a recent outburst after winning a literary prize, Beryl Bainbridge condemned speakers of dialects, including her native Scouse, as ungrammatical. In this she was simply mistaken.

If I now turn to look in a little more detail at the sound system and grammar of so-called Standard English, this is not to assume it is 'more important' or even, nowadays, dominant (US English is the language of world power). It is simply that Standard English or 'RP' is my mother tongue and it has been so well catalogued less than a mile from where I write, at University College London, by A.C. Gimson, following and modifying his famous predecessor, Daniel Jones. (It is said that an earlier phonetician in this distinguished Department was the model for Professor Higgins in Bernard Shaw's *Pygmalion*.) As this book is called *The Poetry of Earth*, in this brief phonetic description I will highlight some features of poetic interest.

At UCL, A.C. Gimson[22] classified the Standard English sound system into twenty vowel phonemes and twenty-four consonant phonemes. The vowel phonemes are:

7 short, which are the vowels: /ɪ/ as in it; /e/ as in bed; /æ/ as in man; /ɒ/ as in hot; /ʊ/ as in put; /ʌ/ as in cut; /ə/ as in the second syllable of sitter.

5 long, which are the vowels: /iː/ as in bead; /uː/ as in food; /ɑː/ as in cart; /ɔː/ as in law; /ɜː/ as in bird.

A colon after a phonemic vowel symbol indicates that it is long.

8 diphthongs (all long), which are the vowels: /eɪ/ as in day; /aɪ/ as in my; /ɔɪ/ as in boy; /əʊ/ as in go; /aʊ/ as in cow; /ɪə/ as in fear; /ɛə/ as in fair; /ʊə/ as in fluent.

Vowels 'colour' the word. A long or a short vowel gives a different quality to a word or group of words. Compare our onomatopoeic representation of rain using all short vowels:

---

[22] A.C. Gimson, *An Introduction to the Pronunciation of English*, 4th edition revised by Susan Ramsaran, (Edward Arnold, London 1989).

'pitter-patter' with that of a donkey long-vowelled braying: 'hee-haw'. Unsurprisingly, all diphthongs are long. In fact, six of our modern English diphthongs were pure long vowels before the Great Vowel Shift, which inaugurated the period of Early Modern English in the 15th century. So, for example our diphthong 'time' /taim/ was pronounced /tiːm/ (like modern 'team') in Middle English.

We can also classify vowels into front and back vowels. Like vowel length, this distinction between front and back gives a different 'feeling' or quality to a word or group of words. Front vowels are formed by raising the front part of the tongue (not the tip or the blade) towards the hard palate. For the closest front vowel the front part of the tongue is raised as close as possible to the hard palate without producing friction (approximately /iː/ as in bead). Gradually the front of the tongue is lowered through half close, half open to the most open front vowel, cardinal 4: /a/, as in Yorkshire /baθ/ = bath. (RP 'bath' sounding like 'hard' is not a front vowel).

Back vowels are formed by raising the back part of the tongue towards the soft palate (velum). For the closest back vowel (approximately /uː/ as in food), the back part of the tongue is raised as close as possible to the soft palate without producing friction. Gradually the back of the tongue is lowered through half close, half open to the most open back vowel: /aː/, which is what the doctor asks you to say when he says, 'Open wide,' (and *is*, approximately, the sound in RP 'bath' /bɑːθ/).

Most Standard English vowels do not exactly fit the four cardinal points (close, half close, half open, open), but they are distinguished on a scale between close and open. In descending order from close to open Standard English front vowel phonemes are: /iː/ as in bead; /ɪ/ as in bid; /e/ as in bed; /æ/ as in bad. Diphthongs which glide to the front are: /ei/ as in bay; /ai/ as in by; /ɔi/ as in boy.

In descending order from close to open Standard English back vowel phonemes are: /u:/ as in boot; /ʊ/ as in put; / ɔ:/ as in bored; /ɒ/ as in pot; /ɑ:/ as in bard. Diphthongs gliding to the back vowel /ʊ/ are: /aʊ/ as in cow; /əʊ/ as in go.

The three central vowel phonemes are /ə/, the nearly always unstressed 'schwa' heard in the second syllable of words like 'butter' and at the beginning of words like 'accept'; a similar but long vowel: /ɜ:/ as in bird; /ʌ/ as in but. Diphthongs gliding to the centre are: /iə/ (fear); /ɛə/ (fair); /ʊə/ (fluent).

It is not necessary to a native English speaker to plot a vowel's position in the mouth to perceive a strong difference in quality between a sentence like: 'The pretty cat creeps in and sits on my lap, then neatly she licks the sweet titbit.' And: 'Cruel laws are hard taskmasters demanding more from the poor.' Obviously, the first sentence has mainly front vowels and the second sentence mainly back vowels. Even if the meaning of the sentence is made as neutral as possible (unlike the above examples), listeners perceive clusters of front vowels as lighter in both senses and clusters of back vowels are both darker and heavier.

It is also interesting the way we compound words like: pitter-patter, zig-zag, knick-knack, sing-song, ping-pong, hee-haw, see-saw, tick-tock, hickory-dickory-dock. The closer vowels come before the more open and the front vowels before the back. This is a form of reduplication, in which the 'echo' slightly modifies the first element. Japanese makes much more frequent use of exact reduplication, often with onomatopoeic effect, such as *gachagacha* = rattle; *chirinchirin* = tinkle; *tobotobo* = plod.

Gimson gives twenty-four English consonant phonemes. Some consonants come in pairs, one voiceless and one its voiced pair. These are the consonants which are formed by completely stopping the passage of air at a particular point in the mouth, or narrowing its passage so as to produce friction. In the list given below the voiceless consonant in each pair is given first and its voiced pair follows it in bold:

Stops:
/p/ /**b**/ pat bat
/t/ /**d**/ to do
/k/ /**g**/ cot got

Fricatives:
/f/ /**v**/ fine vine
/θ/ /**ð**/ thin thine
/s/ /**z**/ sue zoo
/ʃ/ /**ʒ**/ shoe measure

Affricates:
/tʃ/ /**dʒ**/ church judge.

The other English consonant phonemes are the glottal fricative /h/ as in hot; the three nasals: /m/ as in mum; /n/ as in nun and /ŋ/ (never at the beginning of a word) as in sing. Finally there are four 'approximants' or 'semi-vowels': /w/ as in win; /r/ as in red; /l/ as in light and /j/ as in yes.

It is useful to be aware of the consonant pairs, because they are so close and sound very near to full rhymes if they come at the ends of words with the same vowel. For example, 'stop' and 'rob' are much nearer to a full rhyme than 'stop' and 'wrong'. It is also useful to be aware of the manner of articulation of different consonants. For example, we clearly hear the different effect of a group of stops and a group of fricatives: 'Snap, crack, pop, bit' together have an explosive or 'poppy' sound, whereas we feel and hear the friction in 'as if the fifth death were never enough'. Among the fricatives, the group of consonants called sibilants (as in sue, zoo, shoe, measure) have hissy and hushy sounds.

We have gone into some detail about how the small distinctions in the little space of the mouth form the sounds of English, as an illustration of how any language makes so much of so little. English combines a mere forty-four phonemes to produce an enormous vocabulary estimated at over two million words. We can keep on adding to this vocabulary whenever we need to generate a new word. As with the genes that produce such a multitude of individual human faces, we can only marvel at how this discrete combinatorial system of sounds makes infinite use of finite media with such abundant creativity, combined with such economy.

English has its own discrete combinatorial system of grammar, which is not, as some old schoolbooks suggested, a mere application of Latin grammar. Unlike Latin, English is now an isolating rather than inflected system. The English regular verb has only four parts: e.g. walk, walks, walking and walked. We use the same form for 'I walk' and 'they walk'. This means that the subject of the verb cannot be deduced from the verb ending. To mark tenses we bring in many auxiliary verbs, such as parts of the verbs 'be', 'have' and 'do', and modal verbs such as will, would, etc. Thus our past continuous tense is formed with the past simple of the verb 'be': 'was' plus the present participle: 'I was walking'. We use 'will' to mark the future, as in 'he will go'.

As well as being used to form negatives and questions ('I don't want'; 'what do you want?'), parts of the verb 'do' are used as an intensive: 'I do love you.' Instead of repeating the content verb, English may repeat the auxiliary, which acts as an intensive on its own. For example, we could translate Lorca's line: *Ay! qué trabajo me tengo quererte como te quiero* as: 'Oh but it's hard on me to love you as I love you.' But a much more idiomatic translation is: 'Oh, but it's hard on me to love you as I do.'

It has been suggested the regular -ed inflection to form the past simple came from 'did', so that 'walked' might have been 'walk-did'. Like the present tense 'do', the past tense 'did' is still used in past simple negatives and questions and also as an intensive, as in: 'I did go' or 'Oh yes I did'.

Originally Old English nouns had endings as case markers, most of which also fell away. We still use 's' — the same ending as for the plural — to mark both singular and plural possessive case, with very fiddly rules as to where to put the apostrophe, which appear to be falling into disuse. Otherwise we use a mixture of prepositions and word order instead of case endings. Instead of a dative case ending we say: 'She gave the dog to him' or 'She gave him the dog'. Note we cannot say: 'She gave the dog him'. Once verb and noun inflections have been dropped, unlike in Latin, word order becomes more fixed. 'Hugo loves Anna' does not mean the same as 'Anna loves Hugo'.

Superficially, having few inflections makes English a simple-looking language. It is a language in which it is simple to say simple things. But this simplicity is deceptive and covers scope for infinite complexity. There are so many shades of meaning between a whole range of auxiliary and modal verbs. Some of these do duty for indicative and subjunctive inflections and some make finer distinctions. Not only 'do' and 'did' as in the examples above, but all these auxiliaries and modal verbs can stand on their own, with the content verb unexpressed but understood, as in the following persuasive conversation:

'I might but I don't think I should.'
'Why don't you?'

'I ought not to but I would like to. I wish I could.'
'You can. I would if I were you.'
'All right. I will. I may even do it today.'

As well as a whole range of suffixes — such as -able, -ant, -ful — English has a subtle and complex system of phrasal verbs. For example, with 'give' (which alone can mean 'make a present of' or 'budge', as in the case of a stuck jam-jar lid, or a number of other things): 'give in' means deliver an assignment or surrender, 'give up' means renounce (e.g. smoking) or confess an inability to do something (e.g. guess a riddle), 'give over' means transfer or desist, 'give away' means donate, reveal or betray.

To speak a language, we need its set of sounds, we need its grammar and we need its (or some of its) vocabulary. In addition, 'the mystery must be instressed, stressed': we pronounce some syllables more prominently than others. English is stress-timed (more obviously so in England than in the US). That is to say, the time between stresses is, or at least perceived to be, the same, however many unstressed syllables come between. As well as word-stress — meaning which syllable in a word will be stressed rather than another (we say rélative with the stress on the first syllable, not the second or the third) — we have sentence-stress. This goes with the intonation pattern, which conveys a good deal of the meaning of a sentence and gives it its energy and excitement.

Speaking our language is a pleasure. If, to paraphrase Darwin quoted earlier, we regard it as the pleasure in an art for which we have an instinct, we may compare it with other activities for which human beings have an innate potential. Human infants are not born walking but we do not have to teach them to walk. It is a proud moment for the child when he or she lets go of a support and takes a first few staggering steps. We learn to speak with the rhythm, sounds and grammar of our mother tongue.

One of the intriguing things about a language is what Saussure called the arbitrariness of the sign. That is to say, the connection between the word 'dog' and a particular animal is not inevitable. If we take our dog to France, it will be called a *chien* and if we take it to Germany it will be called a *Hund*. It gives one a shock to see a Spanish fast food cafe display the notice: *Perros Calientes*. This is because the term 'hot dog' for a sausage in a bun is a dead metaphor in English and we learn the word *perro* for a live dog in Spanish. It would also make a great difference to a poem if the word 'dog' was replaced by the word *chien* or *Hund*. It might turn a simple little poem about a dog into a kind of *Wasteland*. Speakers of a language develop strong associations and feelings for the words of their language and of course, though the names of things in any language are not inevitable, they do have a history and in that sense they are not arbitrary.

English has a huge vocabulary containing Germanic words from Anglo Saxon, Latinate words via Norman French and from Latin itself at the Renaissance, as well as words from other sources. All these words have their own 'feeling'; for example, words from Anglo Saxon, such as home, eat, drink, love, sleep, usually feel more homely than Latin words. There is a tension between the arbitrariness of the sign and the feel of a word, which we can play with.

Out of the rhythmic excitement of speaking or singing our language, out of enjoyment of its sounds from our mouth, out of associations and feelings for its words, out of the intellectual delight in being able to make and convey meaning through its grammar, comes poetry. We can play with words and their meanings, words and grammar, words and sounds, words and rhythm. We do it for pleasure. Almost every language produces poetry. Poetry, says Wordsworth in his *Preface to the Lyrical Ballads* 'is a homage paid to the native and naked dignity of man, to the grand elementary principle of pleasure, by which he knows and feels and lives and moves.'

Human beings not only walk but dance. Dance is an art, so is poetry. Indeed, García Lorca says that the *duende* — the 'magic' — flourishes best in arts that have a living body as an interpreter — music, dance and spoken poetry. The best poetry does not 'denature' a language but draws on the language's native powers and plays with them. In the old scholastic adage: *Gratia non tollet naturam sed perficit*: 'Grace does not destroy nature but perfects it.'

The rhythmic, phonic, semantic and syntactic wealth and particularity of the language is available for poetry. Traditionally, English poetry had rules about how the first two of these should be used. Old English and some Middle English verse counted stresses and did not bother to count syllables. If there is a fixed number of stressed beats in a line (usually four), this gives a rhythm — with a strong physical rhythmic energy — because English is stress-timed. In addition, the first three of these four beats would alliterate. Later, metres were imported, which counted syllables as well as stresses, and were superimposed on the native English stress-timed rhythm. Thus, an iambic pentameter has five 'iambic feet' of two syllables each, making ten syllables in all, but — much more importantly — one in each 'foot' is stressed, giving five stressed beats to the line. Counting syllables on their own does *not* give a rhythm in English.

As well as rhythmic and metrical complexity, there are many possible kinds of phonic patterning. Old English verse used alliteration but did not usually rhyme at the ends of lines. The possibilities of rhyme — and many degrees of near rhyme — were exploited later. There were rules for various rhyme schemes, such as that for a Shakespearean sonnet. Contemporary poets mainly write in 'free verse' but have all this tradition to draw on to give it strength.

This is a very cursory description of the peculiarities of just one of the four to six thousand languages spoken on Earth. Every other language also has its *own* rhythmic, phonic, semantic and syntactic wealth and particularity, from which it makes its everyday conversation and its poetry. Every language is a unique and uniquely important way to make sense of the world. This is a priceless treasure which must not be squandered. Our mother tongue is the language in which we are at home, which belongs to us and to which we belong, the medium which is our native element.

This does not mean that people necessarily speak only their mother tongue. For example, in Ghana, Nigeria and many other African countries that have a single official language, as many as 90% of the population may regularly use more than one language. Sometimes the majority of the population is bilingual, as in Paraguay where Spanish is the official language and Guaraní is the national language. In Ecuador 40% of the native speakers of an indigenous language are bilingual in Spanish, just as native speakers of Welsh will become bilingual in English if they need to.

In some parts of the world most speakers regularly use both a 'high' and a 'low' version of their language for different purposes, the 'high' when more formal language is appropriate. For example, many Swiss speak both 'High German' *(Hochdeutsch)* and Swiss German; many Arab speakers use both classical and colloquial Arabic and many Greeks use both the high *(katharévousa)* and demotic versions of the language, as the occasion demands.

The same goes for accents. Children who speak Standard English at home with their parents quickly learn to speak with the local accent at school if this is more acceptable to their peers. We all have the experience of speaking in different registers, with different degrees of formality, as circumstances require.

Language and poetry are always crucial in questions of identity, especially if it is threatened. The Kurds have no country, but they have their language, which is essential to preserving their identity as Kurds. Of course, the question of language becomes tangled with the question of national liberation struggles and nationalist conflicts, which is beyond the scope of this book, except to say that the question of language is distinct from the question of nation — many of the bitterest ethnic or nationalist conflicts are between peoples who speak the same language (for example, Yugoslavia and Northern Ireland). In any case, this essay would want to see linguistic diversity preserved even in a world where all nation states had been abolished.

Matthew Arnold said: 'It may cause a moment's distress to one's imagination when one hears that the last Cornish peasant who spoke the old tongue of Cornwall is dead; but no doubt Cornwall is the better for adopting English, for becoming more thoroughly one with the rest of the country.'[23] Even today there are people on the right who think it would be a good idea if the whole world spoke just English. There are also people on the left who think that justice would be served if the whole world spoke one 'non-specific' language; several of these have already been invented but none has 'taken'. One of the main fears that people have of socialism is that it would impose uniformity. That is not a socialism that most of us could ever want. Indeed, a regime that imposed it would be not only unworkable but an intolerable tyranny.

---

[23] Matthew Arnold, *On the Study of Celtic Literature* (first published 1867, Everyman edition, ed. Ernest Rhys, London 1910/76), quoted by Justin Wintle, *Furious Interiors: Wales, R.S. Thomas and God* (Flamingo, 1997), page 42.

Matthew Arnold also inveighed against 'the practical inconvenience of perpetuating the speaking of Welsh.'[24] Against this R.S. Thomas (whose poetry, however, is written in English) laments:[25]

> We are the lost people
> Tracing us by our language
> You will not arrive where we are
> Which is nowhere. The wind
> Blows through our castles; the chair
> Of poetry is without a tenant.

Matthew Arnold was both smug and wrong. The abundance, diversity and particularity of the world's languages adds to the richness and 'poetry of Earth' just as the abundance of species does. And just as many plant and animal species are currently threatened with extinction through the destruction of their habitat, so are many languages.

It has been estimated that half the world's languages will become extinct in the 21st century and only a thousand or so languages will remain in the 22nd century. According to another estimate, 150 (about 80%) of North American Indian languages, 45 Central and South American languages (70%), 45 of the languages spoken in Russia (70%), 225 in Australia (90%) and perhaps 3,000 languages (50%) worldwide are in danger of extinction.

Although not every language can be artificially preserved, any more than every plant or animal species can, this threatened extinction of half the world's languages represents an enormous loss of human treasure, because a language is a medium from

---

[24] *Ibid.*
[25] R.S. Thomas, 'The Lost' in *No Truce with the Furies* (Bloodaxe, Newcastle 1995).

which a culture's poems, stories and songs cannot be extricated. So much of the poetry is lost in translation.[26]

As well as being an enrichment to humanity and the Earth, like the biodiversity of plants and animals, linguistic and poetic diversity is an important insurance against the 'single way of thinking: that of financial capital'.[27] Earlier in this chapter we quoted Stephen Jones describing how languages behave like genes. Drastic cultural and linguistic elimination is as dangerous as the genetic engineering of a single strain of crop — wheat, for example — and allowing other strains to disappear. If the monocrop or monoculture becomes diseased, where can we look for a remedy?

The Nicaraguan poet Ernesto Cardenal has a beautiful poem about some contraband parrots, which had been captured for export to the United States to learn to speak English there.[28] The parrots are rescued and:

When the cages were let open
they all shot out like an arrow shower
straight for their mountains.

Cardenal goes on to say: 'The Revolution did the same for us, I think. It freed us from the cages where they trapped us to talk English...' It comes as no surprise that the US President Ronald Reagan was determined at all costs to exterminate that Revolution.

---

[26] There is no space here to discuss the fascinating problem of translation, especially the translation of poetry, about which we say a little more on page 175.
[27] Communiqué of July 1998 by subcomandante Marcos, quoted in chapter I, page 17.
[28] 'The Parrots' by Ernesto Cardenal is in *Nicaraguan New Time* (Journeyman Press, London 1988), translated by Dinah Livingstone.

Languages may construct the world differently and look at things and relationships from a different point of view. They have a different 'take' on the world and describe it in words with a different 'feel'. However, if as well as their marvellous abundance and diversity, as Chomsky maintains, languages also have an underlying Universal Grammar, 'constructing the world differently' does not mean that these worlds are sealed off from one another. Though it is sometimes so difficult, translation *is* possible. And as we noted above, many people are bilingual or speak several languages as well as their mother tongue.

Speaking another language or struggling to translate can be a pleasure and cannot fail to enlarge the mind. Indeed, with English becoming the dominant world language, native English speakers may end up being the losers, because they will not be forced to learn other languages and therefore be linguistically the poorer. In the Zapatista slogan 'for a world where there is room for many worlds' there is one world — the Earth we share — in which there is room for 'many worlds'.

Likewise, human beings all have a similar human body and human mouth with which to speak their language. Room for 'many worlds' — many cultures, many languages, many poetries — means treating each other with respect and, in Wordsworth's phrase 'the pleasure which the mind derives from the perception of similitude in dissimilitude', which he calls 'the great spring of the activity of our mind.' The respect and the pleasure depend on *both* our likeness and our differences.

CHAPTER III
TIME ON EARTH

What is poetry wording? One approach to answering this large question is through time. If we divide time into past, present and future, the central point is the present. We could say that poetry is wording *presence*. Poetry grasps the particular moment and conveys the feel, the quality of it, as in Blake's 'Auguries of Innocence':[29]

> To see a World in a Grain of Sand
> And Heaven in a Wild Flower
> Hold Infinity in the palm of your hand
> And Eternity in an hour.

Eternity has no past or future; it is only present. Blake's lines echo the scholastic definition of eternity, taken from the philosopher Boethius: *Vitae interminabilis tota simul et perfecta possessio:* 'The perfect possession all at once of life without end.' The most important words are *tota simul:* all at once. The present of eternity holds life *all at once,* sees *all at once:* a world in a grain of sand, heaven in a wild flower.

Much poetry seizes the feel, the mood, the texture of the present moment. Here are two examples. First, the end of Kathleen McPhilemy's poem 'Feel Good',[30] which conveys so well the present moment's 'charge of his energy' transmitted by the horse to herself:

---

[29] In William Blake, 'Poems from the Pickering Manuscript' (c.1803), collected in *Complete Writings* (Oxford University Press, 1966).

[30] In Kathleen McPhilemy, *A Tented Peace* (Katabasis, 1995).

> Here, beside me, a black horse crumples
> rolls over, and again, all the way over
> gets up, fit in his skin, and then
> for no particular reason, or perhaps
> triggered by the sting of the rain, starts forwards
> stops, buckjumps and squeals. The charge
> of his energy reaches the others; together
> like dull thunder, they gallop into the murk.
> And I, too, for no particular reason,
> feel good.

The second example comes from the last section of Mimi Khalvati's book-length poem *Entries on Light*.[31] In a metaphor of startling beauty she describes the moment when she feels a poem 'coming on', which she calls the shining:

> Our own light I mean
>   some sleeping thing
> that rises like a fawn
>   from bracken, half-dazed
> at its own liquidity.

But we are not in eternity; we are in time. The past has gone, the future has not yet come, so the only time in which we are alive is the present moment, just as eternity is only in the present. But unlike the eternal present, our present moment in time is fleeting. In his *Confessions* Augustine has a famous passage meditating on just how fleeting the present moment is. He reflects that first a year, then a month, then a day, then an hour is divisible into past and future moments. He concludes:

---

[31] Mimi Khalvati, *Entries on Light* (Carcanet, Manchester 1997).

If we can think of some bit of time which cannot be divided into even the smallest instantaneous moments, that alone is what we can call 'present'. And this time flies so quickly from future into past that it is an interval with no duration. If it has duration, it is divisible into past and future. But the present occupies no space.[32]

A single moment in time vanishes in an instant. The present moment of 'feel good' or 'shining', which 'tease us out of thought as doth eternity' falls in the twinkling of an eye into the past and is succeeded by a new present moment with a different quality. A poem is an attempt to catch and hold onto that fleeting present, to communicate its presence, to present it. That single moment is not abstract but in time, that is, inserted in a history with a past and future. A single moment can interweave a great deal in a very complex texture.

Anne Beresford is another poet who powerfully conveys the feel of the present moment. For example, her poem 'Instead of Writing to You'[33] sets her mood in the first line, as her mind wanders with the wind to the North Sea — across which her letter must go:

The wind is mournful
tired of worrying the sea into a frenzy
Instead of writing to you
I am thinking of the fishermen
who told me they get cold six miles off shore
they couldn't swim
The one who spoke had brown eyes
not blue
He sold me sprats

---

[32] Augustine of Hippo, *Confessions*, translated by Henry Chadwick (Oxford World Classics, 1991) page 232.
[33] In Anne Beresford, *No Place for Cowards* (Katabasis, 1998).

dead cod in fish baskets
shivered my heart

The poem gives a sense of herself in the present calling to mind someone who is absent, by physically conjuring up the distance between them, a great expanse of cold and dangerous sea. It introduces *other people* into the texture of that present moment. The poem works through the dialectic between the friend's absence, and also his presence to the poet, in the writing of the poem.

Eternity is defined as the duration of that which does not change; time as the duration of that which changes. In wording presence, poetry grasps at eternity, the *tota simul et perfecta possessio*, but because our present is in time, not eternity, poetry expresses the tension between presence and absence, life *tota simul* and death. The pathos of this predicament, the tension of this dialectic generates the poem's energy, which is eternal delight. Even though poetry may aspire to partake of eternity, to:

Hold Infinity in the palm of your hand
And Eternity in an hour

it does so in time, in the physical present moment in time, through the physicality of language produced by a material body. That is why rhythm is so crucial to poetry, because a poem must be *in time* — rhythm, which we first feel from our mother's heartbeat before we are born to spend our time on Earth. That is why in attempting to word presence and communicate it, poetry appeals first to the senses and as Wordsworth says, 'the poet writes under one restriction only, namely, that of the necessity of giving immediate pleasure.' For this, poetic skill and technique are needed as well as the shaping spirit of imagination. One of the qualities with which a poem gives pleasure is beauty. Augustine described the eternity he discovered as 'Beauty so old and so new'.

Wording presence in time applies both to the composition of the poem and to its communication. Of course, the physicality of language in time operates in different ways when the poem is written or spoken. The book and the live speaker present the poem to reader or audience in a different way. The reason, García Lorca says that the *duende* — 'the mysterious power that everyone feels but no philosopher has explained' — is most frequent in music, dance and spoken poetry is that they are arts which 'require a living body as an interpreter — they are forms that arise and die ceaselessly, and are defined by an exact present'. Poetry conveys the *tota simul* of the eternal present by wording presence in time. Poetry embodies eternity in word made flesh, earthly, human language. It speaks in time measured by the human heartbeat, out of a material human body with five senses that will one day die. It is mortal and it holds eternity. As Lorca says of the *duende*, 'it is in fact the spirit of the Earth' — the voice of the one veritable transitory power.

'It can come from the simplest/of things a room/tidied...' says Mimi Khalvati in her *Entries on Light*. Here the starting point of poetry is the physicality of the present moment as it presents itself to the senses. If that present moment is a moment of 'emotion recollected in tranquillity', the emotion is recollected primarily in physical sense-impressions that 'flash upon the inward eye'. But a single present moment contains whole histories, of individuals, families and peoples. They become present in the poem, the poem presents them.

In her poem 'Rubiyat', dedicated to her dead grandmother,[34] Khalvati, who lost most of her native Persian language when she

---

[34] In Mimi Khalvati, *In White Ink* (Carcanet, Manchester 1991).

came to England as a child, uses this Persian form to recall her grandmother, whose world the poet has lost. Both in its form and content the poem is a witness that the absent grandmother and her world are still in some way present to/in the poet. In fact the poem enacts this presence:

> My grandmother would rise and take my arm
> then sifting through the petals in her palm
> would place in mine the whitest of them all:
> '*Salaam, dokhtaré,-mahé,-man, salaam!.*'
>
> 'Salaam, my daughter-lovely-as-the-moon!'
> Would that the world could see me, Telajune,
> through your eyes! Or that I could see a world
> that takes such care to tend what fades so soon.

Comparably, in a very different setting, the dialectic in Seamus Heaney's poem 'Digging'[35] is between his association with and distance from his family's generations of great peat diggers in Ireland:

> By God the old man could handle a spade.
> Just like his old man.
>
> My grandfather cut more turf in a day
> than any other man on Toner's bog...
>
> But I've no spade to follow men like them.

Having escaped from this hard labour by engaging in intellectual work, the poet 'quarrels with himself' about whether he has broken a heroic tradition and become less manly than his forefathers. The last verse of the poem revolves back to the first

---

[35] In Seamus Heaney, *Death of a Naturalist* (Faber, London 1966).

verse and to the present. The pen he is holding is also a tool, he says:

> Between my finger and my thumb
> the squat pen rests.
> I'll dig with it.

In this (perhaps insecure?) resolution, the poet's forefathers remain present in the poet, as the family history of digging continues into the present with the present poem.

Heaney is just one of many poets who have written country poems evoking memories of his childhood. Time is cyclical and proceeds in seasons, which have always concerned poets; indeed one of the earliest types of poetry, liturgy, usually draws on the seasonal cycle. In the Introduction to his anthology, *Scanning the Century*,[36] Peter Forbes, the editor of *Poetry Review*, says: 'In a secular and highly mobile age, the timeless repetition of seasons and religious rites have lost their force,' so poems about nature, the country, weather and season are no longer 'in'. This somewhat fatuous urban prescriptiveness makes one wonder whether Forbes thinks we have become disembodied. What does he think we eat?

> Still it is turning.
> *Eppur si muove*
> The twelve-spoke wheel of moons

is how Michael Hamburger begins his book-length poem *Late*.[37] It is disputed whether Galileo uttered his famous words about the Earth: *Eppur si muove* — 'it *does* move' — on his deathbed or immediately after signing his forced recantation. Hamburger's use of them not only honours Galileo's stand against the Inquisition

---

[36] Peter Forbes (ed.), *Scanning the Century* (Penguin Viking, 1999).
[37] Michael Hamburger, *Late* (Anvil Press, London 1997).

of his day, but refutes the trivial trendiness of a millennial editor by producing a marvellous evocation of the turning seasons and the lives of countless flowers, trees, animals and birds progressing through them. But the poem is much more than this. It is *Late* because late capitalism has done so much damage to the Earth and its creatures:

> *Civitas?* Dead Latin.
> The word for it now is market,
> Money's global playground
> Where mutilations, carryings-off
> Occur as a matter of course.
> The referees have their orders
> From the prompters of Presidents,
> From the High Priests of profit.

It is also late in the century and the poet's life. We live our life through the cycle of the seasons, year in year out, but from birth to death our lifetime is linear. Now aged over 70, the poet reflects on coming towards the end of the line. But it is a lifetime full of other people:

> Late, now to see at all,
> Lines, colours, shapes grown familiar,
> Yet, looking, see those lost.
> Listening, hear absent voices
> And acknowledge the new...

Some of these relationships are very long-standing as in the section about a love that was 'Tried by difference, division,/Adventuring, too, the trial/Interrupted by separation.' This section ends:

> Where also we may meet
> As at first we were

> In dream that rewinds
> The wanderings, the weathers,
> City-scapes, landscapes a moment creates and wipes out;
> And emerging once more from those transmutations
> You, made more present by every absence,
> I see as at first you were.

Hamburger's poem *Late* is his greatest work to date, because of its scope, embracing nature and history, the seasonal cycle and the linear time both of a personal life and world political events, in passages ranging from lyric beauty to prophetic rage. It is interesting that Forbes's dismissal of nature and the seasons in his introduction to his *Scanning the Century* is accompanied by an uncritical acceptance of 'American pre-eminence': 'Whatever is to come it was the American century.' Is it possible that poets who keep their feet on the ground and stay in tune with the seasons see more clearly the damage this US-dominated neoliberal market is doing to the Earth? Liturgy and epic are two of the oldest forms of poetry. Is there any connection between the jettisoning of the seasons with their liturgical cycle, and the death of epic by the self-proclamation of the end of history through the triumph of US-dominated late capitalism?

The quality of presence in a poem is intensified when it is a conversation in a tradition — both a literary and a historical tradition (we hear the echoes of Thomas Hardy in the last quotation above from *Late*). The present of the poem may not only recapitulate the past but embrace the future. The 'now' of the poem both recovers memories –– in which personal and collective are interwoven — and envisions a utopia. For example, Arnold Rattenbury's 'Edward Thomas Walking'[38] contains many echoes of Thomas's work while developing Rattenbury's own concerns, walking the heady Welsh hills where Thomas walked:

---

[38] In Arnold Rattenbury, *Living Here* (Katabasis, London 1996).

Holiday women and men
and children sprung from a prison Now
to a past Then or future Then:
political dreamers perhaps
that scribble poems, contour philosophers' maps...

All temptations on Earth lie fresh in the sun
below like a land Planned
and Promised. Everything's possible.
The mist has gone. We understand

everything. There it lies,
itemised, News from Somewhere, and at hand.

As well as connecting with Edward Thomas — with an epigraph from him heading this section: 'Except William Morris there is no other man I would sometimes like to have been' — these lines use the temptation of Christ[39] and William Morris' *News from Nowhere* in a subtle conjugation of faith and illusion. The final section of the poem, which begins with the line 'And then at war he died', comes down firmly on the side of faith and against the assertion that poems 'make nothing happen':

But he had walked and seen
and swooped on what could startle into being
matter impervious
to gunshot: seeds all safely sown
in the soil of language...

And nor can we foretell
how on this creeping Earth seed is to swell
to a harvest of certainties...

---

[39] Matthew, chapter 4.

Infinitesimal things like his

immediate footloose poems change
and are huge as a lofty political vision is.

The power of a poem depends not only on the impact of its images, its delicate workmanship and linguistic ingenuity, but on the strength of its historical roots — its conversation, including in the older sense defined by the OED as 'the action of living or having one's being in or among' — and the scope and quality of its vision. The more it embraces both past and future *tota simul* — all at once — the more the present of the poem holds eternity. The presence the poem is wording will be more luminous, not because it covers a longer time-span or contains more material, but because it participates more fully in the scope and quality of the presence of eternity: *Vitae [interminabilis] tota simul et perfecta possessio:* the perfect possession of life all at once.

Poems are written out of many traditions. In earlier chapters we stressed how 'the poetry of Earth' comes from the intractable particularity of its many species, cultures, languages and of course this is true of poetry itself. Particular voices speaking out of particular histories with their own proper names are the stuff of poetry. Wole Soyinka is a Nigerian poet who has spoken out bravely against the dictatorship in his own country. In his poem 'New York. U.S.A.',[40] having made the same journey across the Atlantic as many African slaves before him, but in his case by air, he describes his disorienting arrival at the airport in New York, where 'This gash of smiles does not promote/my ease .' Then when he takes the filthy subway through 'Manhattan's bowels,/Bronx and Brooklyn, Harlem, Queens ... Mammon's sated belly' he summons great figures in the history of the

---

[40] In Wole Soyinka, *Mandela's Earth and Other Poems* (André Deutsch, London 1989).

struggle for black rights and indeed for all workers, Mammon's underbelly:

> With every wombward rip and its unanswered
> Scream, remember Bessie Smith. Remember
> Muddy Waters, Leadbelly, Sojourner Truth,
> Recall that other Railroad Underground.
> Remember why the Lady Sang the Blues,
> Remember, yes, the Scottsborough Boys,
> The sweet-sad death knell of Joe Hill.

With the rhythm of the train all these figures are present in the poem of the African poet's underground journey beneath New York. By re-presenting them, the poem bears witness to Joe Hill's assertion in his 'death knell': ' I never died, said he.'

Soyinka writes in English, but the poetry of Earth is in many languages speaking out of many traditions. This means, if we want to look at a few more examples from other traditions, for the purposes of this essay they have to be translations. Because particularity is the stuff of poetry, often 'poetry is what is lost in translation', so the translated examples need to be read with some imaginative compensation as translations. Recently, outside the House of Lords, who were about to announce their ruling on General Pinochet's extradition to Spain, people on the picket were chanting:

*Se siente, se siente
Allende está presente.*

The translation unfortunately loses both rhythm and rhyme: 'we feel it, we feel it, Allende is present.' But the Spanish chant had extraordinary power, as supporters and Chileans who had been exiled more than a quarter of a century, summoned Allende to be present at the moment when the fascist general who had overthrown him, killing and torturing so many, might at last be brought to justice. There was a strong sense of Allende's presence; the chant was *performative*.

The Chilean poet María Eugenia Bravo Calderara was a university teacher in Santiago at the time of the coup which overthrew President Allende. After imprisonment and torture she escaped to England and only saw Chile again in 1990. Then she re-visited the house of Pablo Neruda, who died shortly after the coup:

> And I swim, go under, go down
> to the oldest depths of my bones.
> I feel the blood running through my veins,
> through dark forests of araucarias...
>
> and through you, your house,
> your books, at once
> I arrive at my origins.
>
> I too am this.
> This meeting point
> and through your house,
> your books, your Araucana
> I can speak to Don Alonso
> and tell him:
>
> 'In this country the war is still going on.'[41]

Looking back in 1990 at the long-term psychological damage inflicted by the coup on her generation of young activists, even if they survived it, she writes in her pointedly brief poem 'Image', here quoted whole:

---

[41] From María Eugenia Bravo Calderara, 'Voyages' in *Prayer in the National Stadium*, translated by Dinah Livingstone (Katabasis, 1992).

> When we were learning lately
> to see ourselves in the mirror
> know who we were and where we came from
> the military arrived and had their coup.
>
> They raided, arrested and killed.
>
> And the worst of it was
> they not only took the mirror away
> but they also broke it.

The Nicaraguan experience has been very different from the Chilean and so is their poetry. In 1979 they overthrew a dictator. They tried to create a fairer society on the side of the poor and for eleven years they resisted the violent opposition of the US, enraged by the 'threat of a good example' in what it regarded as its own backyard. Fifty thousand died in the struggle to get rid of the dictator and many thousands more in the war against the US-backed Contras. At ceremonies in Nicaragua it was the custom to call out the names of their heroes and martyrs and for the assembled people to respond to each name: *Presente!:* Present!, as to a roll call. (This was the context in which the Pope caused such enormous offence on his visit to Nicaragua in 1983 when he refused to mention the names of those killed the previous day in a Contra attack, whose mothers were at his Mass.)

Nicaragua's most famous poet, Ernesto Cardenal, became Minister of Culture and in the early euphoric years immediately after the Revolution he recalls the guerrilla poet Leonel Rugama, who was killed in a famous shoot-out with the National Guard in 1970. Rugama's poem 'The Earth is a Satellite of the Moon'[42] was written shortly after the US astronauts trod on the moon in 1969

---

[42] Leonel Rugama, 'The Earth is a Satellite of the Moon' in *Poets of the Nicaraguan Revolution*, translated by Dinah Livingstone (Katabasis, 1993).

and left their footsteps in its thick dust. Before becoming a Sandinista guerrilla, Rugama had been a seminarian studying for the priesthood in Managua and frequently used to go for walks in a very poor district of the city called 'Huellas [Footprints] de Acahualinca', because prehistoric footsteps were preserved there in volcanic rock. Rugama's poem, which has some fine comic touches, compares the mounting cost of the Apollo flights with the mounting poverty of the people of Acahualinca. The poem ends: 'Blessed are the poor because theirs shall be the moon.'

After the triumph of the Revolution, Ernesto Cardenal's poem 'Final Offensive'[43] ends by addressing Leonel Rugama and 'updating' his poem:

The moon was the Earth. Our bit of Earth.
and we got there.
                And now Rugama
it's beginning to belong to the poor; the Earth is
(with its moon).

Cardenal's poem begins: 'It was like a trip to the moon' and throughout it describes the Final Offensive in terms of a moonshot. It is a conversation with Rugama's well-known poem. By telling Rugama about the Final Offensive that saw off the dictator, Cardenal's poem makes him, who never lived to see that day, *Presente!*

In another poem, 'Elvis', Cardenal dreams that Elvis, one of the members of his peasant community in Solentiname who was killed in the Assault on San Carlos Barracks in 1977, has not been killed and is showing the poet his new baby. Cardenal is a Catholic priest who cannot marry and have children, which he sometimes seems to find very hard. The poem ends:

---

[43] In Ernesto Cardenal, *Nicaraguan New Time*, translated by Dinah Livingstone (Journeyman, London 1989).

>   Then I awoke and remembered you are dead
> and your isle Fernando is called
>   Elvis Chavarría now
>   you can no longer have
>   that new child to take after you,
> any more than can I
>   you are dead like me
>   although we are both alive.

Ernesto Cardenal's Ministry of Culture set up poetry workshops all over the country, in which participants both read and wrote poetry. Lesbia Rodríguez, one of the workshop poets, wrote a poem reflecting some lines from a pre-Revolution poem by Edwin Castro, 'Tomorrow, my child, everything will be different.'[44] Lesbia begins her poem: 'Everything is different.' Then she addresses her unborn child:

> And you, child, who are still in my womb,
> I stroke you with my hands brushing my belly
> and talk to you about the future...

> And I will take care of you as our soldiers
>   take care of the Revolution.
> And you will grow and fill the land with your children.
> And I will be older
>   and Nicaragua younger.

The pregnant woman sitting in the park inserts herself in her people's history, conversing with former poets in her tradition and conversing with her unborn child as she looks to the future.

---

[44] Lesbia Rodríguez, 'Reflection upon Reading a Poem' in *Poets of the Nicaraguan Revolution*.

On a larger scale, Ernesto Cardenal inserts the Sandinista Revolution into his epic poem 'Quetzalcóatl', which belongs to his *Homage to the American Indians*. His later 581-page *Cántico Cósmico* is literally cosmic in scope.

The first issue of *Poesía Libre,* the Ministry of Culture's poetry magazine, included a translation of 'Song of the Nicaraguas',[45] a Nahuatl poem about the Spanish conquest:

> When the sun sets, my lord, my lord,
> my heart hurts, it hurts ...
> Day-fire do not go away,
> fire do not go.
> The sun has gone.
> My heart cries.

The obvious suggestion of its publication in *Poesía Libre* number 1 was that the night was over. In 1990 the Sandinistas were defeated by the US-backed UNO alliance. On the morning of the election results, Vice-President Sergio Ramírez relates how, in the street where they both lived, he met the poet Ernesto Cardenal sitting in the gutter weeping. For them once again:

> The sun has gone.
> My heart cries.

After the Sandinista defeat, the poet and former Interior Minister Tomás Borge addressed the people of Europe in Madrid in 1990:

> Although Europeans retain their cultural heritage, they prefer for the most part the expensive and dehumanising trinkets of consumerist society. Citizens of the old continent, I invite you to step out of your gloom. You have

---

[45] In *Poets of the Nicaraguan Revolution*.

conquered everything, but all you have gained is individual isolation. Now it is your turn to discover for yourselves a sense of community with all humankind.

He reaffirms his faith in a 'philosophy of liberation, concerned with an integrative and kindly humanism, which considers the liberation of humanity as the basic objective of culture.' This, he says, 'is the finest utopia ever conceived in the history of Latin America: the new human being.' This new humanity 'will conquer Europe not in order to colonise it but in order to liberate it, so that its own mythical ceremonies can be initiated afresh and rise again from their solemn and wonderful burial ground.'

The great modernist poem *The Wasteland* describes this solemn and wonderful burial ground. It is more convincing about destruction, death and depression than in its positive elements. The 'fragments shored' and the 'falling cities' are much stronger in the poem than the attempted resolution in the Sanskrit mantras at the end. These have an air of being tacked on — from an unassimilated, imported culture — and therefore 'unearned'. Many readers find the *Shantih Shantih Shantih* easy-preachy and irritating. If it can be regarded as a resolution, it is the wrong one, an evasive, quietist one.

Nevertheless, its modernism is still seeking some kind of restored wholeness. Postmodernism does not even try to put the fragments together; it revels in a knowing and 'ludic' pick-and-mix. It is the perfect partner to the dominant triumphalist neoliberal New World Order, which does indeed consider it has 'conquered everything' and therefore reached the end of history, so that 'grand narrative is dead, socialism is dead, utopia is dead'. Postmodernist 'playfulness' is based on these assumptions. Just as capitalism suppresses the damage it does — the human agony and danger to the planet — postmodernism wilfully ignores them. Wars happen 'on television'. That is not real blood, real pain, real hunger, real death: it is an 'image', a 'text'. Postmodernism has lost all sense of urgency, even any sense of the future. In this it is a hideous distortion of the 'eternal present', because rather than *tota simul*, it is 'a little bit of this, a little bit of that and nothing matters more than anything else': bus ticket and Bible are both 'texts', a fashion show and a massacre are both 'media images'. This kind of multiculturalism, picking and mixing texts and images from all over the world — gutting and repackaging them — to offer the jaded consumer fun and frisson — goes hand in hand with 'the imposition of one single way of thinking: that of financial capital,' which 'implies the destruction of humanity as a sociocultural collective and reconstructs it as a market place.'[46]

Certainly, the English radical tradition is buried at the moment. A fine poet writing in this tradition, like Arnold Rattenbury quoted above, is marginalised. The New Labour government has done its utmost to cut its links with its radical past. *Poetry Review* is not the only magazine to employ writers with little interest in this tradition and possibly little knowledge of it. For example, when I read some of *Samson Agonistes* (announcing the title) at a poetry reading in London, a reviewer for *Poetry London Newsletter* came up to me afterwards and asked: 'Did you write that?' I replied: 'No, Milton did.' She said: 'I thought it sounded a bit antique!'

A great tradition coming down from before Langland and the Peasants' Revolt in 1381, through Tyndale, greatest of all English translators who translated the Bible for 'ploughboys' and was burnt for it (no poet can rely on a biblical allusion being picked up by readers today), through Milton and the countless superb writers of the English Revolution, through Blake, Wollstonecraft, early Wordsworth and Coleridge, Shelley, William Morris and onward — to name but a few — is now underground or merely

---

[46] Communiqué of July 1998 by subcomandante Marcos, quoted in chapter I, page 17.

tapped to perform in fancy garden-centre toy fountains, as featured on TV. They are the past. Seriously conversing with them is certainly not the way to 'get on' in the poetry world. Not only the past, but any utopian vision of the future has also been marginalised.

However, on Easter Saturday 1999, on the 350th anniversary of the Diggers of the English Revolution, who began their digging on St George's Hill on April 1st 1649, a small procession marched to the Hill and erected a memorial stone there. Gerrard Winstanley, the Diggers' leader, was a liberation theologian and speaks of 'Christ rising again in the sons and daughters'. St George's Hill is now a very affluent golf course and erecting this stone there on Easter Saturday was a small act of resurrection, contradicting the current strictures against the seasons, on the one hand, and politics on the other, as subjects for poetry. The Diggers began their digging at Eastertime on 1st April, and here is Gerrard Winstanley, whose words have much more in common with Tomás Borge and the Zapatista Marcos quoted earlier[47] than with current fashionable English poetry editors:

> When the Earth becomes a Common Treasury again... then this enmity in all Lands will cease, for none shall dare seek a dominion over others, neither shall any dare to kill another, nor desire more of the Earth than another; for he that will rule over, imprison, oppress and kill his fellow creatures, under any pretence soever is a destroyer of the Creation and an actor of the Curse.

> [So] the work we are going about is this, to dig up George's Hill and the waste ground thereabouts, and to sow corn; and to eat our bread together by the sweat of our brows. And the First Reason is this, that we may work together in

---

[47] See chapter 1, page 17.

righteousness and lay the foundation of making the Earth a Common Treasury for all, both rich and poor.[48]

Or as he writes to General Fairfax:

The truth is, experience shows us, that in this work of Community in the Earth and the fruits of the Earth is seen plainly a pitched battle between the Lamb and the Dragon.[49]

However 'uncool' it is to mention it, that pitched battle is still going on.

This chapter has argued that poetry intensifies its presence according to how far it *embraces* past and future, that is, according to the strength of its historical roots — how it converses in a tradition — and the scope and quality of its vision. English poetry needs its tradition, and the scope and quality of its vision needs that tradition's radicalism. Nevertheless, if strong roots are the basis of the one veritable transitory power, we should note that that power is double-edged. Just as the power of poetry, particularly its performative power can be for good or ill, the danger of being rooted in beloved soil is a murderous nationalism.

Recently, in the week that the Home Secretary was saying Middle England would not tolerate many more asylum seekers and toughening the controls on them, a large group of local citizens of Leeds, including many pensioners, made a huge banner and held it up to the sky to greet an incoming plane-load, saying: WELCOME KOSOVANS. In a television programme on

---

[48] *A Declaration to the Powers of England and to all the Powers of the World* (1649) in Gerrard Winstanley, *Selected Writings* (Aporia Press, London 1989).
[49] *To the Lord Fairfax, General of the English Forces and his Council of War* (1649) in *Selected Writings*.

'Englishness' broadcast that same week, viewers were asked whether they thought of Englishness as 'independence and self-reliance' or as 'openness and tolerance'. In the passages quoted from Winstanley above, we see *both* these sets of qualities: on the one hand the Diggers are bent on self-determination, and on the other, and they are unfailingly *internationalist*.

> For the Earth, with all her fruits of Corn, Cattle, and such like, was made to be a Common Store-house of Livelihood to all Mankind, friend and foe, without exception.[50]

The best of the English radical tradition is patriotic but *internationalist* and conversing in this tradition today includes discerning and criticising it.

A tradition is not 'pure', just as there is no such thing as 'racial purity'. Traditions can combine like the discrete combinatorial system of genes, which produces each distinct individual person. True multiculturalism is not the dead hand of knowing and ludic postmodernism but 'the inclusion of different societies [and individuals] incorporating their particularities'. There are many other traditions besides the English in England. One only has to attempt to count the number of languages spoken in London. If you live in London you are a Londoner.

Following the biblical book of *Revelation*, Blake's vision of a future society where justice and peace reign is a *city*, is *London*. In the English pastoral tradition, the rural is the place of innocence. Blake's vision of London as Jerusalem sees the 'politics of innocence', not as a going back but a going forward, a future creation. Wordsworth looked to 'sermons in stones, books in the running brooks' but the *city* is where people can undergo the most radical change. (For William Morris in *News from Nowhere* the

---

[50] *A Declaration from the Poor Oppressed People of England* (1649) in Gerrard Winstanley, *Selected Writings*.

transformed London is a *garden city.)* Nationalism usually appeals to a *country,* as in the hymn, with its seductively sweet melody:

> I vow to thee my country
> all earthly things above
> entire and whole and perfect
> the service of my love.

In this hymn the perfect society is *deferred* to an other-worldly heaven: 'And there's another country/I've heard of long ago...' This kind of nationalism goes together with alienation.

For Blake the transformed society must be in *this* world or nowhere. In one section of his poem *Jerusalem*[51] he combines both a vision of the heavenly city coming *down to Earth* in a transformed London and the forces operating against it. Jerusalem's golden pillars stand on 'the fields from Islington to Marybone/To Primrose Hill and Saint John's Wood and:

> Pancras and Kentish Town repose
> Among her golden pillars high
> Among her golden arches which
> Shine upon the starry sky.

> The Jew's harp-house and the Green Man
> The Ponds where boys to bathe delight,
> The fields of cows by Willan's farm
> Shine in Jerusalem's pleasant sight.

The enemy forces are those who 'take advantage':

> Is this thy soft Family-Love,
> Thy cruel Patriarchal pride,

---

[51] *Jerusalem* (1804-1820).

Planting thy Family alone
Destroying all the World beside?

But in Jerusalem the Earth will become a Common Treasury, not only of real estate but hearts and minds:

In my Exchanges every Land
Shall walk, and mine in every Land
Mutual shall build Jerusalem
Both heart in heart and hand in hand.

People writing out of their different traditions want to keep them alive; they do not want to be curiosities, colourful tourist knick-knacks or fodder for social workers. They want a community in which to converse, and maybe also skilful translators to reach others who do not speak their language. One of the benefits of the city is cultural exchange and just as mixed marriages produce new combinations of genes, so traditions combine in new distinct poetic voices.

For example, the poet A.C. Jacobs comes from a family of Lithuanian Jews who settled in Glasgow. Here is his complete poem 'Place':[52]

'Where do you come from?'
'Glasgow.'
'What part?'
'Vilna.'
'Where the heck's that?'
'A bit east of the Gorbals
in around the heart.'

---

[52] In A.C. Jacobs, *Collected Poems and Selected Translations* (Hearing Eye/Menard Press, London 1996).

Both his Jewishness and his Scottishness are core elements in this poet's work. Of course, all poets are free to borrow from whatever they want, but their work is stronger if they write out of what they are and where they come from. The poetry of Earth is the immense diversity of landscape, species and cultures with all their different languages to talk about it.

Poetry itself, in the commonest sense, is the soul of any language because it is the most intense, the most economical, the most beautiful wording of presence. Like all the countless species of birds with their different songs, all over the world countless voices make poetry in their own languages, out of their own histories and traditions, in all their discrete combinations. Alive and truthful to their experience, these infinitely subtle and varied tones modulate the voice of the planet. This chapter began with Blake's 'Auguries of Innocence':

To see a World in a Grain of Sand
And Heaven in a Wild Flower
Hold Infinity in the palm of your hand
And Eternity in an hour.

Another reason why Blake is a great writer in the English radical tradition, rather than the other-worldly gnostic some have misrepresented him as, is that the next two lines of the poem, intimately connected with the opening lines above, are:

A Robin Red breast in a cage
Puts all Heaven in a Rage.

This is the Blake who was a friend of Tom Paine and may have helped him to escape to France. The *tota simul* of the Eternity in his poem embraces the Robin Red breast in a cage and rages at it. Many poems have been written in prison. 'The day when all people treat each other as equals will be the day when revolution will have been perfected in this savage and contradictory world,' says Tomás Borge, whose poem to his two-year-old daughter, 'Letter to Ana Josefina',[53] was written in prison. In that prison he famously promised his gaolers and torturers (and fulfilled his promise when he became Sandinista Interior Minister after the Revolution):

> My personal revenge will be your children's right
> to schooling and to flowers...
>
> My personal revenge will be to offer
> these hands you once ill-treated
> with all their tenderness intact.

The captives will be freed. Their sighing and sobbing will be over. At the dawn chorus on that utopian morning, the uncaged Robin Red breast will be present, opening wide its beak to utter its thrilling silvery song, and all the birds of the air.

---

[53] Translated in *Poets of the Nicaraguan Revolution*, as is Tomás Borge's 'Revenge' that follows.

CHAPTER IV

DOWN TO EARTH

1

THE POETIC GENIUS

AND THE SPIRIT OF PROPHECY

In the beginning of Time, the Great Creator Reason made the Earth to be a Common Treasury, to preserve Beasts, Birds, Fishes and Man, the Lord that was to govern this Creation, for Man had Domination given to him over the Beasts, Birds and Fishes; but not one word was spoken in the beginning that one branch of Mankind should rule over another.

And the Reason is this, Every single man, Male and Female, is a perfect Creature of himself.[54]

This is the beginning of Gerrard Winstanley's justification of the Diggers' action on St George's Hill in 1649. As England at the time was a Christian culture, it was natural that the political struggle should be expressed in Christian language. But in this great anti-hierarchical, anti-imperialist claim to 'Community in the Earth and the fruits of the Earth', he does not speak about God, but the 'Great Creator Reason'. His purpose in doing so is not

---

[54] Gerrard Winstanley and others, *A Declaration to the Powers of England, and to all the Powers of the World, shewing the Cause why the Common People of England have begun, and gives Consent to Dig up, Manure, and Sow Corn upon George-Hill in Surrey* (April 20th 1649).

only theological but *political*: to justify the poor Diggers' political action in digging up St George's Hill in order to feed themselves. In the English radical tradition the de-supernaturalising of God has gone hand in hand with the struggle for justice and political liberation. Over the centuries liberation theology becomes humanism. This tradition continues to this day. There is no room to trace its whole history here, but we can give just one more nineteenth century example and then look back in a bit more detail at its double nature in William Blake.

At great personal cost, Emma Martin, who had been a strict Baptist, renowned for her debating powers, bolted from her Baptist husband and joined the Socialists in 1839 to become a feminist and freethinker. She continued to speak on the same platforms, on which she had previously bashed her Bible, *against* the oppressive Christianity she had formerly defended, and in support of those she had formerly attacked. George Fleming spoke about her at the Owenite Congress of 1841:[55]

> On looking at the position of woman, she had seen that all remunerating employment was taken from her, that all institutions were confined to males... She saw no remedy for this till she saw the remedy of Socialism. When all should labour for each, and each be expected to labour for the whole, then would woman be placed in a position in which she would not sell her liberties.

Now we go back fifty years to William Blake. In his posthumous book on Blake, *Witness against the Beast*,[56] E.P. Thompson traces the links in the English radical tradition connecting Blake to the writers of the English Revolution. In his prose piece 'All

---

[55] Quoted in Barbara Taylor, *Eve and the New Jerusalem* (Virago, London 1984).
[56] E.P. Thompson, *Witness against the Beast* (Cambridge University Press, 1993).

Religions are One', subtitled 'The Voice of One Crying in the Wilderness', Blake argues:[57]

Principle 2nd: As all men are alike in outward form, so (and with the same infinite variety) all are alike in the Poetic Genius.

Principle 5th: The Religions of all Nations are derived from each Nation's different reception of the Poetic Genius, which is everywhere called the Spirit of Prophecy.

Principle 6th: The Jewish and Christian Testaments are an original derivation from the Poetic Genius...

Principle 7th: As all men are alike (though infinitely various) so all Religions etc., as all similars, have one source.

The true Man is the source, he being the Poetic Genius.

Principle 2nd is akin to Chomsky's Universal Grammar, underlying the world's thousands of languages. *Principle 5th* is saying that the Poetic Genius is the source of all religions, which differ because Nations receive it differently. Religions are poetic creations and the Poetic Genius is also 'everywhere called the Spirit of Prophecy'. That is to say, one of the functions of poetry is to speak out. *Principle 6th* includes the Jewish and Christian Testaments — religions — as products of the Poetic Genius, human inventions. In *Principle 7th* all religions have one source because all men are alike (though infinitely various).

Like Wordsworth a few years later,[58] Blake is praising likeness in difference, here language as a human universal, together with the

---

[57] c.1788. William Blake, *Complete Works* (Oxford University Press edition 1966).
[58] In *Preface to the Lyrical Ballads,* 1800 edition.

multiplicity of different languages. Likewise, all religions have one source — the Poetic Genius — although there are many religions, cultures, poetries, which are all human creations. The fact that there are many different 'receptions' of the Poetic Genius throughout the world enormously enriches the poetry of Earth. This is part of the human treasury, but, as Blake says in his *Marriage of Heaven and Hell*,[59] religions have been used for oppression:

> The ancient Poets animated all sensible objects with Gods or Geniuses, calling them by the names and adorning them with the properties of woods, rivers, mountains, lakes, cities, nations, and whatever their large and numerous senses could perceive.
>
> And particularly they studied the genius of each city and country, placing it under its mental deity;
>
> Till a system was formed, which some took advantage of, and enslaved the vulgar by attempting to realise or abstract the mental deities from their objects: thus began Priesthood; choosing forms of worship from poetic tales.
>
> And at length they pronounced that the Gods had ordered such things.
>
> Thus men forgot that all deities reside in the human breast.

Blake praises the many different 'receptions' of the Poetic Genius as human wealth and abundance. He includes religions among the creations of the Poetic Genius. This abundance is not in itself dangerous but wonderful. The ancient poets did not invent but tried to *discern* what 'their large and numerous senses could

---

[59] *The Marriage of Heaven and Hell* c.1790-93.

perceive.' Hence they animated 'all sensible objects' with Gods or Geniuses, which was a way of naming the nature and powers of these objects: natural objects, such as woods, rivers, mountains and lakes; and cultural entities, such as cities and nations. Woods, rivers, mountains and lakes are *real* natural resources, which people fight over. Cities and nations have *real* powers of life and death. So the poets were not telling fairy stories but trying to discern the forces that operate in and govern the world. Religion becomes a system of oppression to 'enslave the vulgar', when it attempts to 'realise or abstract the mental deities from their objects' — that is set them up as idols, access to which is controlled by priests.

Blake's common term for an oppressive system that 'enslaves the vulgar' in order to maintain control in the hands of a few, is Mystery. 'Pity would be no more/if we did not make somebody poor' begins the frightening poem 'The Human Abstract'.[60] It goes on to describe the process by which religion is used to gain control:

Soon spreads the dismal shade
Of Mystery over his head:
And the Catterpillar and Fly
Feed on the Mystery

Creating the Mystery is the way in which 'some took advantage' by abstracting or supernaturalising (i.e. claiming that natural forces are actually supernatural) *real* natural and cultural forces in order to enslave others. 'And at length they pronounced that the Gods had ordered such things. Thus men forgot that all deities reside in the human breast.' The supernaturalising or alienation of these forces, the seizure of control of them by some in order to enslave others turned the forces into Nobodaddy, that is, an idol

---

[60] *Songs of Experience* c .1789-94.

with powers of human sacrifice. As Blake puts it in his poem 'To Nobodaddy':[61]

> Why darkness and obscurity
> In all thy words and laws,
> That none dare eat the fruit but from
> The wily serpent's jaws?

In an additional poem to his *Songs of Experience*, Blake describes the dark side of human nature as 'A Divine Image':

> Cruelty has a Human Heart,
> And Jealousy a Human Face;
> Terror the Human Form Divine
> And Secrecy the Human Dress.

He fulminates against human injustice in many of his other poems, not only against the 'priests in black gowns... walking their rounds,/and binding with briars my joys and desires.' In 'Holy Thursday'[62] he attacks child poverty, which is still widespread in England today:

> Is this a holy thing to see
> In a rich and fruitful land,
> Babes reduced to misery,
> Fed with cold and usurous hand?
>
> Is that trembling cry a song?
> Can it be a song of joy?
> And so many children poor?
> It is a land of poverty!

---

[61] *Poems from the Notebook*, 1793.
[62] In *Songs of Experience* c. 1789-94.

However, the pair to both 'The Human Abstract' and 'A Divine Image' in his *Songs of Experience* is 'The Divine Image' in his *Songs of Innocence*[63] (and we note that this time the Divine Image has a *definite article*):

For Mercy has a human heart,
Pity a human face,
And Love, the human form divine
And Peace, the human dress.

Then every man, of every clime,
That prays in his distress,
Prays to the human form divine,
Love, Mercy, Pity, Peace.

Blake is saying that human beings contain both the terrors of 'The Human Abstract' and the qualities of 'The Divine Image'. There is a battle between them, just as in his poem *Jerusalem* the beautiful city comes *down to Earth,* to real London. Pancras and Kentish Town repose but the repose is threatened by 'cruel patriarchal pride/planting thy family alone/destroying all the world beside.'

***

Don Cupitt's book *After God*[64] echoes Blake in describing religion as a creation of the Poetic Genius. 'The historic function of the entire supernatural world of religion was to represent to us the world of linguistic meaning — a world that has always been curiously difficult to enter and think about except through poetry

---

[63] *Songs of Innocence,* 1789.
[64] Don Cupitt, *After God* (Weidenfeld and Nicholson, 1997). In this section all Cupitt quotations are from *After God* or his latest work, *Kingdom Come in Everyday Speech* (SCM Press, 2000).

and myth.' Or as he puts it in a later chapter: 'Through its system of supernatural beliefs, a society represents to itself the way that its language builds its world.'

He gives a fascinating account of how religion developed to match the development of human society. In a threefold historical analysis, first, he describes how for human hunter gatherers the universal class of animal they were hunting was a spirit. 'It would help the hunters to reify the kinds that they hunted, in spirits or totems that they could, as it were, hold before their eyes as they searched... The reindeer spirit is a picturesque way of thinking the concept 'reindeer, the class term, the common noun.' In addition, spirits are like the place names on a map: 'they make the world more interesting and negotiable.'

Cupitt argues that philosophy was a secularisation of much older — and often religious — patterns of thought: 'Demythologised spirits turn out to be general words, and the huge power of the spirit world over the world of sense experience turns out to be the huge power of language to form, order, and classify reality... the supernatural world of religion is a metaphorical — and indeed, a mythical — representation of the world of language.' 'The Paleolithic hunter called this thing that guided him a spirit, Plato calls it a Form, Kant a concept, and I call it just a word.'

Second, Cupitt agrees with Blake that the god of a city-state was a human creation, concerned with control, including control of meaning, and that the function of priesthood was to help maintain this control. He sees spirits as typical of the old nomadic order and belief in gods as emerging with the development of agriculture and the first settled state societies from about 8000-7500 BC. 'Towns and cities then follow, each city having as its principal building a temple dedicated to its patron god.' This god is seen as having unified and set in order not only the city-state but the cosmos. He becomes the focus of a cult, maintained by a college of priests. 'Whereas spirits are a mobile and rather unpredictable lot [like the hunter gatherers themselves], a god's throne is established forever and his cult is established forever. He is immortal.' This divine being is 'a townie', set 'at the heart and centre of the man-made realm of culture:'

> One may see the god as being something like the spirit of the state; he or she was a sign of its unconditional and even cosmic authority.

At the third stage, which Cupitt dates at about the time of Abraham, God becomes personal with a capital 'G', 'because then the whole divine order was called to account by the individual, and in the form of a person.' This coincided with 'the emergence of a more individuated human selfhood standing in a new relation to the world.' 'God,' he suggests, 'began with the possibility of questioning God. God and human subjectivity were born more or less together, and God has ever since functioned as the mirror in which we look to become ourselves.' But this personal God is still a human creation, 'an imaginary personification of the whole scheme of things, and the one who is to be loved, praised, thanked, grumbled about, argued with, questioned.' The analysis traces the human creation of supernatural beings appropriate to the stage of human development, and these supernatural beings mirror the human beings at each stage.

Cupitt is a distinguished heir of half the English radical tradition: its struggle to de-supernaturalise God. But he squanders the other half of his birthright for a mess of postmodernism, when he ignores or jettisons de-supernaturalisation's unfailing accompaniment in this same tradition: the struggle for political liberation and justice. His latest book, *Kingdom Come in Everyday*

Speech,[65] seems to assume the 'kingdom' has come. Given that the central message of the Sermon on the Mount is: 'Seek first the kingdom and its *justice*[66] — τὴν βασιλείαν καὶ τὴν δικαιοσύνην αὐτοῦ — and all these things shall be yours as well',[67] it is extraordinary that in this book, the word *justice* barely figures at all.

For Cupitt, religion is 'an experiment in selfhood', 'a set of attitudes and techniques' or tricks for self-development. When he speaks of salvaging what was valuable in religion after de-supernaturalisation, he picks out three themes, which he calls the Eye of God, the Blissful Void and Solar Living. These are all ways of pursuing 'our own personal growth by exploring and flipping among several different forms of selfhood and views of life.' They are about Me.

Kingdom Come's style is happy clappy — of the urbane Cambridge kind, rather than mid-West tele-evangelist. The book's keynotes are individualism and privatisation, its salient characteristic is massive complacency. Cupitt's theme is a 'morality of lifestyle, "pride" and free self-expression', because 'personal faith is privatised.' According to him, 'the world-wide triumph of liberal democratic politics [brings us] to the end of history.' For 'the democratic process is an historical achievement that *has* no "beyond"... fully-developed liberal democracy is already post-historical. Liberal democracy is kingdom politics... The whole globe is becoming democratised: it is becoming a theatre and a market that never shuts.'

The proclamation of the Kingdom, declares Cupitt, was a 'self-fulfilling prophecy' and 'there has already occurred a rather extensive "realisation" of Christian eschatology'. There are 'a

---

[65] *Kingdom Come in Everyday Speech* (SCM Press, London 2000).
[66] Or: 'Seek first [God's] kingdom and his *justice*.
[67] Matthew 6:33.

whole series of structural resemblances between... the world of our postmodernity and the traditional ideal world-at-the-end-of-the-world that religion has called the kingdom of God.' Cupitt says rather tetchily that if anyone makes objections to this, 'either they rest upon a misunderstanding or I have already replied to them.' He regards himself as unassailable and has become a priest of the neoliberal New World Order, endorsing it with far more elegance and grace than a mid-West tele-evangelist can command.

Cupitt asserts that 'the whole cosmological or grand narrative side of religion has totally collapsed.' It is not true that just because there is no supernatural God in heaven, the struggle for justice on Earth has become pointless. In fact, the opposite is the case. If God, in Cupitt's phrase, is 'the religious ideal — that is, a unifying symbol of our common values', then de-supernaturalising God means bringing that ideal *down to Earth*. Bringing God down to Earth to 'reside in the human breast' is not Kingdom Come (although it helps). Kingdom Come means first justice — on Earth, because we have no other world. Even if we never reach utopia, never fully succeed in creating a reign of justice and peace in the world, the point is not to give up trying. This is a pilgrimage. This is a grand narrative, which the death of God has not destroyed but reinforced.

'Religious conservatives,' says Cupitt, 'used to assert that one must not permit the objective reality of God to be questioned, because the death of God would inevitably be followed by the death of Man and the death of the world. They were correct.' Cupitt is not in the least worried at the prospect. This is the basis for his support for triumphant global capitalism. It is a basis which cannot stand, because it ignores the reality of what is going on in the world today.

Against this, the Zapatista sub-comandante Marcos, stresses in his communiqué[68] that in financial capital's 'war of conquest everything and all of us are subjected to the criterion of the market — anything that opposes it or presents an obstacle will be eliminated'.

Marcos takes for granted that the survival of humanity *matters*. Speaking both on behalf of the other, the Indian, the excluded, who — it is patently obvious — abound all over the world, and of humanity as a whole, he issues this dire warning about the neoliberal global market:

> It implies the destruction of humanity as a sociocultural collective and reconstructs it as a market place. Opposing neoliberalism, fighting against it, is not just one political or ideological option, it is a question of the survival of humanity.

Cupitt proposes: 'If we can't beat postmodernity, we should embrace it'. His postmodernism leads him to assert that 'nothing is deep'. But it is not true that because everything has a history, including linguistic meanings, the result is 'universal melt-down, nihilism, postmodernism'. It is easy to see why postmodernism is the ideal philosophical companion to the massively unjust neoliberal New World Order, because it is simply unconcerned with the reality of suffering and injustice in the world. 'Instead of a faith,' says Cupitt, there is 'whatever one is currently "into"... instead of society, the market and one's own circle.' As he puts it in *Kingdom Come*: 'In postmodernity we are no longer worried, because we do not believe in progress any more.'

Back in the real world, the struggle for justice continues. To return to just one recent example from abroad[69] on January 21st

---

[68] See chapter I, page 17.
[69] See chapter I, page 12.

2000, the indigenous peoples of Ecuador and their supporters rose up against the proposed dollarisation of the economy and took over the Parliament building in the capital, Quito, to install a 'poncho utopia' trying to create justice in their country. These indigenous peoples see this as a new phase in a five-hundred-year-old historical struggle, which is *by no means over.*

This uprising was rapidly defeated by big business and US pressure, but as Antonio Vargas, one indigenous leader, puts it: 'Our road is long, it does not come to an end in one day, and this was an advance along the road,' or as another leader, Blanca Chancoso, says: 'This uprising is like giving birth. It has just begun but when the *guagua* (baby in Quechua) is born they will see how strong it is.'[70] Throughout the Third World, the idea that we have already reached the 'end of history' is either meaningless or, if true, a disaster.

In *Kingdom Come* Cupitt is excited by the Human Genome Project as 'some indication of what people might opt for when they have a free choice in the matter.' This is a world away from the reality of biopiracy in the Third World. As we saw,[71] many samples of Ecuadorian indigenous blood were stolen (apparently, by members of US Pentecostal sects) to put on sale in US Genome Boutiques and on the internet.

Cupitt assumes that postmodernism has brought about the end of idolatry. But the opposite is the case. Mammon is an idol, which demands countless human sacrifices every day, far more than any of the old religions. It is the only idol that Jesus condemns by name in the Sermon on the Mount: 'You cannot

---

[70] The quotations in this paragraph and the next are from Kintto Lucas, *We will not Dance on our Grandparents' Tombs. Indigenous Uprisings in Ecuador* (CIIR, London 2000).
[71] In chapter I, page 12.

serve both God and Mammon.'[72] Cupitt says: 'It is very curious that God and Mammon should have changed places ethically. Mammon is internationalist. He wants people to be healthy and well educated. He wants peace and stability, progress and universal prosperity.' He praises the multinational companies: 'It is conventional to criticise the multinationals for being mobile, rootless, anonymous, and interested only in profit, but I'm pointing out that it is *precisely these features* that make them morally superior to our old locally based national and religious identities.'

When we look at the enormous suffering and damage caused by global capitalism, particularly in the Third World, these remarks are fatuous. Mammon does not care at all whether people are healthy and well educated, except when it suits it. Mammon is massively involved in wars and the arms trade, rather than peace and stability. In the last twenty years the gap between rich and poor has widened enormously in England, as well as all over the world. Mammon creates haves and have-nots, rather than universal prosperity. Cupitt's remark about multinationals that: 'Being mobile and global, they cannot afford to operate by generating and excluding an "other"' is the opposite of what actually happens to millions of poor and excluded people all over the world.

'It is very postmodern,' says Cupitt, 'suddenly to realise that we no longer actually need roots, identity, stability or provenance. We can do without all those things. Me, I don't want them anymore.' Firstly, it is somewhat comic that a retired Cambridge don, with many unmistakeable characteristics of a retired Cambridge don, rooted in English philosophy and that pleasant way of life, should regard himself as having no identity. Perhaps he thinks of this as a kind of norm or default identity, just as the

---

[72] Matthew 6:24.

neoliberal global market's 'single way of thinking, that of financial capital' thinks of itself as the triumphant norm.

Perhaps that is unfair to Cupitt, but speaking in praise of 'the end of the other', he gives a telling list of 'much the same syllabus' schoolchildren are studying all around the world: *'English,* mathematics, science, and technology.' English first on the list speaks volumes. In Ernesto Cardenal's poem 'The Parrots'[73] some contraband parrots have been captured for export to the United States 'to learn to speak English there.' The parrots are rescued and:

> When the cages were let open
> they all shot out like an arrow shower
> straight for their mountains.

Cardenal goes on to say: 'The Revolution did the same for us, I think. It freed us from the cages where they trapped us to talk English.' President Ronald Reagan, who waged a genocidal war to exterminate that Revolution, is bizarrely included by Cupitt in *Kingdom Come* in a chapter on 'postmodern saints'.

The Zapatista slogan *Por un mundo donde quepan muchos mundos:* 'for a world in which there is room for many worlds' means the opposite of the end of the other. The poetry of Earth is the particularity, abundance, diversity and gratuitousness of all life on Earth and the Zapatista slogan means the *inclusion* of the other in the enjoyment of Earth's rich bounty.

Don Cupitt praises globalisation and the end of the other, because he considers it superior to ethnic and tribal rivalries causing endless wars. (This is the argument put to the 'savage' in Huxley's Brave New World.) In the first place, with globalisation

---

[73] Quoted in chapter II, page 49.

and the hegemony of the neoliberal New World Order, we have not seen an end to wars: they have become even more horrible in their 'collateral damage', not to mention their poisoning of the Earth. Secondly, even when ethnic and tribal rivalries are a factor in causing wars, they are never the only factor and seldom the principal factor. Economic factors are nearly always involved, such as the struggle to control resources, often between rival powers or 'princes', who may succeed in manipulating and mobilising ancient tribal loyalties or may use conscription or mercenaries. In wars of the 1990s (including, it was suggested recently, NATO's bombing of Kosovo?) access to oil has been a major factor.

Obviously, in our world today, problems of religious tribalism are far from solved, but it is untrue that neoliberal capitalist globalisation solves such conflicts by causing the 'end of the other'. The 'end of the other' is a euphemism for enormous suffering and death and also a huge irreplaceable loss of the poetry of Earth. Neither is it true that all ethnic groups, tribes and nations want to exterminate others. Many indigenous religions are concerned with the survival of their own way of life and looking after the Earth for the sake of *all humanity*.

***

The Poetic Genius is 'everywhere called the Spirit of Prophecy', meaning that poetry must speak out, bear witness, unmask idols. The confrontation described by Marcos for humanity against neoliberalism is dramatically expressed in the great poetry of the 'Harrowing of Hell' in *Piers Plowman*.[74] After his death on the cross Christ descends into Hell to release the captives and confronts Lucifer at the gates of hell:

---

[74] William Langland, *Piers Plowman*, Passus 18, c.1377 (i.e. four years before the Peasants' Revolt).

Thou art Doctor of Death, drink that thou madest.
I that am Lord of Life, love is my drink
and for that drink today I died upon Earth.

When the Poetic Genius speaks as the Spirit of Prophecy today it must be against the Doctors of Death currently operating in our world. The Latin American liberation theologian Jon Sobrino defines an idol as *a false god that demands and feeds on death* — Blake's Nobodaddy. It is simply not true that there are no invisible powers operating in the world and controlling lives. We have only to think of the Futures Market. As Christopher Hampton puts it in his poem about a pleasant pub lunch in a sunny London street:[75]

And at such moments one could be forgiven
for supposing London's teeming lunchtime air
was freely ours — not bought or fought for...

Yet all the time, containing us, the abstracts
are at work that keep us all on leash.

Even if a poet today does not speak in terms of gods or idols, Nobodaddy or Mammon, the Spirit of Prophecy is still needed to study the genius, that is, discern these powerful forces and name them for what they are.

If religion is a creation of the Poetic Genius, then like all poetry its 'one veritable transitory power' can be used for good or ill. 'Poetic tales' of gods can be used to prop up a dominant oppressive world order or to subvert it. Thus religion becomes a poetry of politics, a symbolic way of talking and acting politically. Religions also have histories; they become a tradition with which their adherents identify and which thereby gives these adherents a

---

[75] Christopher Hampton, 'The Leash' in *Against the Current* (Katabasis, 1995).

significant part of their identity. These religious groups, in their turn, then become political forces. There will be a political struggle for *ownership* of the tradition — the 'poetic tales' of the supernatural god, the mixture of myth and historical fact in the life of the founder and the story of the religion from the time of the founder to the present day.

A clear example of this is the present-day Catholic Church in Latin America. On the one hand, there is the Church which preaches the God of the powerful imposed on indigenous people of the Continent by the conquistadors. On the other, there is the Church of liberation theology which proclaims the God of the poor. (The first line of the Nicaraguan *Misa campesina* is: '*Vos sos el Dios de los pobres:* You are the God of the poor.') Both sides insist that their God is the God of Jesus Christ. In fact these two 'Gods' are like two opposing forces, so there is a struggle between their adherents for ownership of the true God of Jesus Christ.

From his side of the world, Jon Sobrino agrees with Blake that: 'Where Mercy, Love and Pity dwell/There God is dwelling too.' He also shares a vision of 'Jerusalem', for which he uses the New Testament term 'kingdom' or 'reign of God'. Sobrino's monumental *Christology* seeks to establish what the historical Jesus was like, because of his concern for 'the crucified people' in Latin America. This is where Christ is to be found on Earth now. 'It is the crucified people who make Christ's passion present today, those who fill up in their bodies what is lacking in Christ's passion.'[76] 'The crucified people are Christ's crucified body in history'. Sobrino describes the horrific massacre by the Salvadorean army at Sumpul in 1980.[77] He goes on to say:

---

[76] Jon Sobrino, *The Crucified Peoples,* (CIIR, London 1989), page 3.
[77] *The Crucified Peoples,* page 2.

Sumpul is the new name for Golgotha. Thousands of peasants journeyed to this river and died there; some were drowned, others shot by the army. For them it was the end of a much longer journey, which they had taken every day of their lives, during which they had been dying bit by bit through desperate poverty and exploitation. There are many other Golgothas like Sumpul.

He continues:

The victims weep. Archbishop Romero says: 'This is hell's empire.'

Like Jesus they are crucified by the 'sin of the world', the 'structural sin' of the poverty and death inflicted upon them by the powers that rule the world. In their hope and their struggle for life they are 'rising again'.

Sobrino is in no doubt whatever that the central Christian message is: 'Seek first the kingdom and its justice — τὴν βασιλείαν καὶ τὴν δικαιοσύνην αὐτοῦ.'[78] 'We have to announce God's kingdom in the presence of the anti-kingdom ruled by idols and in opposition to them.'[79] Idols are false gods that demand and feed on death and the chief idol today is Mammon, worshipped by global capitalism. Sobrino is clear that the kingdom and its justice are to reign *on Earth*. This kingdom or 'reign of God' is the core of liberation theology. Unlike Cupitt, he is under no illusion that the kingdom has already come: 'It is the reality of Latin America today and of the Third World in general that calls for a reign of God... The major fact in Latin America is the massive, unjust poverty that threatens whole populations with

---

[78] Or: 'Seek first [God's] kingdom and his justice': Matthew 6:33.
[79] Jon Sobrino et al., *Santo Domingo and After* (CIIR, London 1993), page 30.

death. At the same time, the most novel fact is the hope of a just life, of liberation.'[79]

For Sobrino and his fellow liberation theologians, this is the gospel. As a Jesuit, Sobrino remains within the constraints of orthodox Catholicism (though he is surely pushing against them in expressions such as 'God who has become history').[80] But his whole concern is with bringing the kingdom and its justice down to Earth. God the Father acts as a sort of principle, an ideal, 'the God of life', that must be realised on Earth: *gloria dei vivens homo:* the glory of God is the human being alive. Sobrino seems much more interested in Jesus than in the Father and Jesus is to be found today in the crucified people.

Sobrino strongly disagrees with Bultmann that Jesus' death at the hands of the political authority was 'a tragic mistake'. The basic accusation against him was, Sobrino says:

> Jesus wants to destroy the temple. In this religious formulation Jesus is implicitly but unambiguously accused of seeking the radical subversion of society. The temple was the symbol of the totality of society in the religious, economic, financial and political areas. Jesus was therefore a prototype martyr (from *martyrion* = witness) to the kingdom of God.

In his essay on the Santo Domingo Bishops' Conference of 1992, Sobrino quotes the *Secunda Relatio* of the Latin American bishops (suppressed by Rome in the Conference's final published Document):

---

[79] Jon Sobrino, 'Central Position of the Reign of God in Liberation Theology' in I. Ellacuría and J. Sobrino (ed.) *Mysterium Liberationis* (Orbis Books, New York 1993), page 356.
[80] *Santo Domingo and After,* page 40.

On 24th March 1980 the Church and world opinion were appalled by the horrible murder of the Archbishop of El Salvador, Oscar Arnulfo Romero, who fell riddled with bullets while celebrating mass, a martyr to the episcopal ministry because he acted like a prophet.

Nearly ten years later in the same city of San Salvador on the night of November 16th 1989, six Jesuit priests of the Central American University, together with two women domestic workers, were cruelly massacred in their home by soldiers during the curfew. The news again shook the world: they died for their commitment as priests and religious [monks and nuns] to justice and respect for human rights.[81]

Archbishop Romero was killed in his own cathedral shortly after denouncing the army and the death squads from his pulpit: 'I ask you, I implore you, I order you: Stop the killing.' The six Jesuit priests were Sobrino's colleagues.[82] He only escaped because he happened to be abroad that night. Like Jesus, these and countless others in Latin America were 'martyrs to the kingdom of God'.

The *Secunda Relatio* continues:

[This persecution] is happening within the western Christian church and perpetrated by those who claim to be defenders of this culture and Christian principles. It is happening because the various idolatries oppressing the Continent, which were denounced at Puebla [Bishops' Conference] have felt threatened.

These 'various idolatries' have fought back by:

---

[81] *Santo Domingo and After,* page 31.
[82] See Jon Sobrino, *Companions of Jesus: the Murder and Martyrdom of the Salvadorean Jesuits* (CIIR, London 1990).

the spreading and financing of sects propounding a spiritualistic and uncommitted religiosity, by supporting a liberal individualist Christianity and also by direct attack and persecution.

As Sobrino goes on to say later:

> To give a single example, the Atlacatl battalion [financed and trained in 'counter-insurgency' techniques by the US], which is known to have committed the El Mozote massacre and the murder of the Jesuits in El Salvador, among other things, still brandishes its slogan proclaiming 'For country and with God'.

This slogan would have been familiar to the conquistadors. In his *Preaching of the Gospel to the Indians,* written in Lima, Peru in 1577, the theologian José de Acosta describes 'the third category of barbarians':

> This is composed of savages resembling wild beasts... and in the New World there are countless herds of them... They differ very little from animals... It is necessary to teach these people who are hardly men or who are half men... They must be held down by force... even against their will, they must be compelled to enter the kingdom of heaven.[83]

Or in the words of the Maya prophet Chilam Balam de Chumayel:[84]

---

[83] Quoted by Enrique Dussel in 'Modern Christianity in Face of the "Other"', *Concilium* 150, 1979.
[84] Quoted by Enrique Dussel in 'The Real Motives for the Conquest', *Concilium* 1990/6, page 42.

It was only because of the mad time, the mad priests, that sadness came among us, that Christianity came among us; for the great Christians came here with the true God; but that was the beginning of our distress, the beginning of the tribute... the beginning of fighting with firearms, the beginning of the outrages, the beginning of being stripped of everything, the beginning of slavery for debts.

In his work, *The Devastation of the Indies*,[85] the Dominican friar Bartolomé, de Las Casas tells a story showing that the Indians thought the god of the Christians was gold:

A cacique... called Hatuey ... said to them, 'Now you must know that they are saying that the Christians are coming here... because they have a god they greatly worship... You see their God here.' He had basket full of gold and jewels and said, 'You see their God here, the God of the Christians.'

Las Casas endorses this view:

Their reason for killing and destroying such an infinite number of souls is that the Christians have an ultimate aim, which is to acquire gold, and to swell themselves with riches in a very brief time.

Millions vanished during this genocide in the name of Christendom. It has been estimated that in 1492 in what is today Latin America and the Caribbean there were 100 million people. By 1570 there were no more than 10-12 million. In that century the populations of England and Spain were about 3 million each. As Gustavo Gutiérrez has said: 'Trying to cover up the witnesses of the time to the immense destruction of persons, people and

---

[85] Bartolomé de Las Casas (1484-1566), *The Devastation of the Indies: A Brief Account* (New York 1974). Quoted by Enrique Dussel.

cultures, together with their vital links with the natural world, is like trying to cover the sun with one hand.'[87]

Gutiérrez is writing in a special issue of the theological review *Concilium*, entitled *1492-1992: The Voice of the Victims*. In their editorial to this issue Leonardo Boff and Virgil Elizondo say:[88]

> In Abia Yala (an indigenous name for Latin America, which means 'mature land') peoples already existed 40,000 years ago. Great cultures grew up here, with bodies of sages, sophisticated understanding in astronomy, agriculture and medicine and with elaborate languages and religions. All this was considered the work of Satan. Christianity... was implacable and ethnocentric when confronted with cultural difference. The 'other', the indigenous person, the black person, was regarded as the enemy, the pagan, the infidel.

The Christendom model of Christianity which satanises the 'other' persists today both in one form of Latin American Catholicism and in the increasing number of Protestant sects whose missionaries come from the US to preach the 'American way'. Fundamentalist Protestants preach a quietist conformism that offers no resistance to the neoliberal New World Order, whatever the scale of suffering and death this imposes on their would-be converts and so many others. As Pablo Richard says:[89]

> *Death faces the indigenous peoples today exactly as it has ever since 1492.* Genocide continues in countries like Guatemala... The natural environment where they live is destroyed, and

---

[87] Gustavo Gutiérrez, 'Towards the Fifth Centenary', *1492-1992: The Voice of the Victims, Concilium* 1990/6, page 2.
[88] V. Elizondo & L. Boff, Editorial, *Concilium* 1990/6, page viii.
[89] '1492: The Violence of God and the Future of Christianity', *Concilium* 1990/6, page 65.

the Earth raped. Worst of all they are continually humiliated, marginalised, discriminated against, banned, as peoples, races, ethnic groups and cultures. The dominant churches, for their part, continue to be European, western and white; any sign of the growth of an Indian church is banned and checked. Indigenous liturgy is banned. Indigenous religion is relegated to the sidelines.

The violence against the 'other' not only continues but the capitalist global market is accelerating it. In chapter I, we mentioned some examples, including the Yanomami of the Amazon whose home, health and very existence are threatened by the invasion of goldminers. We quoted from the 'Declaration to all the Peoples of the Earth' by Davi Kopenawa Yanomami.[89] The Declaration continues:

> Our way is better than that of the whites because we preserve the rivers, streams, lakes, mountains, the game, the fish, the fruit — cabbage-palm, bacaba palm, the nuts, cocoa, cocoawood, wine-palm, what already exists, what Oman created.

When Pope John Paul II visited Peru, various indigenous groups presented him with an open letter which contained the following passage:[90]

> John Paul II, we Andean and American Indians, have decided to take advantage of your visit to return to you your Bible, since in five centuries it has not given us love, peace or justice.

---

[89] Boa Vista, Roraima, 28th August 1989, duplicated. Quoted in *Concilium* 1990/6, page 82.
[90] Quoted by Pablo Richard in 'The Violence of God and the Future of Christianity', page 67.

Please take back your Bible and give it back to our oppressors, because they need its moral teachings more than we do. Ever since the arrival of Christopher Columbus a culture, a language, religion and values which belong to Europe have been imposed on Latin America by force.

One of the distinguishing marks of liberation theology in Latin America is that slowly it is learning to respect the 'other', rather than exterminate or suppress them. In his essay on the Santo Domingo Bishops' Conference of 1992, Jon Sobrino says:

However difficult it is to recognise the 'poor' it is even more difficult to recognise the 'other', even though frequently both coincide in the same person or group... The 'other' really introduces us not only to what is different but to the unknown... Out of shame and responsibility, something serious had to be said about indigenous and blacks on the fifth centenary.[91]

As Bartolomé, de Las Casas had said five hundred years previously: 'If we were Indian we should see things differently.'[92]

A crucial 'other' is, of course, between male and female, the source of so much poetry. This can take an oppressive form with the male as 'default' and the female as deficient 'other' or a celebratory form of creative sexuality. The ancient Mexican creator god was called Ometecutli-Omecíhuatl, the Lord and Lady of Duality. The Mexican liberation theologian María Pilar Aquino's book *Our Cry for Life*[93] voices some demands of women,

---

[91] Jon Sobrino in *Santo Domingo and After*, page 38.
[92] Quoted by Gustavo Gutiérrez in 'Towards the Fifth Centenary', *Concilium* 1990/6, page 3.
[93] María Pilar Aquino, *Our Cry for Life: Feminist Theology from Latin America* (Orbis Books, New York 1993).

including that liberation theology itself should listen better to women. In the same essay on 'the other', Sobrino recognises: 'As for the matter of women, it is also evident that we cannot continue as we have up till now.'

As Boff and Elizondo stress in their editorial to this 5th centenary issue of *Concilium:* 'Recognition is essential, since it embodies the minimal justice we owe to these "others."'[94] Liberation theology, says Pablo Richard, is trying to replace the colonial Christendom model, 'whose actions and theology brought about the massacre of the Indians and Afro-Americans on our continent.'[95] The first principle in this struggle is: 'defending the lives of the indigenous peoples'.

The beginning of this chapter discussed how, in the English radical tradition, the de-supernaturalisation of God has gone hand in hand with the struggle for justice and political liberation. Although Latin American liberation theologians do not explicitly de-supernaturalise God, nevertheless the criteria by which they discern whether even the God of their own Church is a God of Life or an idol are *humanist* ones: human life, especially endangered human life, and the life of the Earth. So in a different way, through their theology of Incarnation — Christ is to be found on Earth today in the 'crucified people' — they also bring God *down to Earth*. A God, even a so-called Christian God, who is a God of Death, not a God of Life, is an idol.

Recognition of the 'other' means not trying to impose on them, leaving them the space (including the physical space) to do things in their own way. In chapter I we looked at some examples of the world's threatened indigenous peoples struggling to survive and maintain their cultural identity, in which their religious ceremonies are very important. Among them, we saw how the

---

[94] *Concilium* 1990/6, page viii.
[95] Pablo Richard, page 64.

remaining Huichol people are trying to maintain their culture and religion with the deer, maize and peyote as their divine trinity. As with the Yanomami, their sacred ceremonies are intended to help look after *the whole Earth* (and it is true that their way of life does not over-exploit the Earth as the loggers and miners do). The Huichol go on pilgrimages to get the peyote, from which the sacramental mescalin gives shaman and people the 'enlarged and numerous senses' to produce their sacred visions:

> They are the songs of peyote.
> They are memories of Viricota
> sung by the gods of Viricota.[96]

On the other hand, as chapter I also pointed out, just because a culture or religion is 'ethnic', this does not automatically make everything about it indiscriminately good. We quoted Ernesto Cardenal's poem *Quetzalcóatl,* which condemns the Aztecs for their human sacrifices and describes how the 'antifascist' resistance to the Aztec rulers, the Tlamatinimes, kept alive the teaching of Quetzalcóatl, the ancient god-king, who had been driven out of the city for forbidding human sacrifices. He had 'taught children how to live': they must strenuously avoid evil and 'a human being must be honoured like a precious stone and rich plumage'. So, among the Aztecs, says Cardenal, these Tlamatinimes developed a 'Quetzalcóatl liberation theology'.

The last two lines of his long poem are:

> Quetzalcóatl, or the historicity of myth.
> Carrasco calls him subversive.

Like the myth of the 'once and future king', or indeed the Christian story of Paradise Lost and Paradise Regained, the future

---

[96] 'Eight Huichol Shaman Poems', in *Flower and Song* (Anvil Press, 1977).

Jerusalem, the Quetzalcóatl liberation theology looked back to a mythical good time to inspire them to look forward to a future time of justice and peace on Earth, when the good ruler would return. It was tragic that when the Mexicans saw the Spanish conquistadors coming from the sea, they welcomed them as the returning Quetzalcóatl.

Likewise, today, indigenous peoples are developing their own liberation theologies. In the Kuna language, says Aiban Wagua:

> This is called *pabgan e nagkannar nudaked*[97] (dust, clean, polish, perfect, set out and make useful the legacy of our ancestors)... This will redouble our will to self-determination as peoples, convinced of our richness and our duty to make a special contribution to our brothers and sisters who suffer like us. This will bring about *a more human world for all,* in fellowship with nature, our mother Earth.

As he goes on to say, 'one part of the Church is on our side... it struggles together with us and also dies together with our people who fall. Another part of the Church is aggressive.'

We have taken examples from Latin America, but obviously it is possible for every religious tradition to develop its own liberation theology *against human sacrifice.* A religious tradition is a symbolic and poetic way of representing the whole range of human potential and activity — for good or evil, for life or death. The task of the Spirit of Prophecy in each tradition is discernment. This is comparable to what happens with the individual human person. Each of us has the capacity for kindness and for murderous rage, as well as many other things, and we have to

---

[97] In 'Present Consequences of the European Invasion of America', *Concilium* 1990/6, page 55.

select from all this human material and potential how we want to act and what we want to become. Vices and virtues are habits.

If we regard religions as creations of the Poetic Genius, the religion as well as all the other poetry produced by every culture is part of humanity's great treasury in all its abundance, diversity and particularity. As well as religions each needing their own liberation theology to defend human life, the core of any humanist ethic must also be *against human sacrifice*, which is still just as prevalent today as in the past. Humanism also needs poetry, poetic ways of living and ceremonies. And diversity in all of these. As with biological species, diversity is a safeguard in case a dominant monoculture becomes corrupt. Just as liberation theology seeks first the kingdom and its justice and then all these things shall be yours as well, so the core of humanism is *respect for human life* and then all the abundant diversity of the poetry of Earth will be ours as well.

One of the last Aztec poems[98] written when the Spaniards were beginning their wholesale suppression of the indigenous culture of Mexico in 1521 concludes:

> They have abandoned the capital already.
> Smoke rises, the mist
> is spreading.
>
> Weep, my friends,
> and know that by these deeds
> we have forever lost our heritage.

Today the violence of the capitalist global market against the 'other' is more powerful than the 'proudest arms of Spain'. The violence is real, not 'non-real', not only in Latin America, but

---

[98] Translated in *Flower and Song* (Anvil Press, 1977).

globally. This is the reality of the 'end of the other' which Don Cupitt celebrates as postmodernist lightness of being. His endorsement of the current hegemony is as cavalier as that of the conquistadors and most of their attendant clergy.

The Aztec word for poetry is *in xóchitl in cuícatl:* 'flower and song'. 'They came to make our flowers wither, so that only their flower might live,' was how the Maya prophet Chilam Balam de Chumayel described the 'end of the other' perpetrated on his continent by the conquistadors — as in Blake's *Jerusalem:*[99]

> Planting thy Family alone
> Destroying all the world beside.

The word 'anthology' means a collection of flowers. The poetry of Earth's glory is that it has so many different flowers and so many different songs.

---

[99] Quoted in chapter III, page 73 and in this chapter above, page 84.

2

THE HUMAN FORM DIVINE

Incarnation and Trinity

Religion can be both a form of social control and *social poetry* expressing people's aspirations towards what they lack, 'the sigh of the oppressed', not just as individuals but as a society. Theology and liturgy are poetic attempts to articulate a particular society and also what that society *lacks*. Articulating *lack* is inherently subversive, so the powers-that-be may go to great lengths to control this subversive tendency by deferring the satisfaction of that lack, the fulfilment of these needs and desires, to another world, to which they hold the keys. The social poetry of religions creates rituals to express the life of a society as it is — often celebrating a seasonal cycle — and articulates aspirations, which the controllers of the society (ruler and priest, who may be one) vet and may punish as heresy. Which of the prophets did not your fathers persecute?

A secular society still needs poets and prophets. As well as articulating and to some extent creating our world, language — and poetry in particular — is also needed to *discern* its controllers, its ruling spirits or forces. Many people are disappointed with the Millennium Dome and what it is expressing about us. Many people were depressed by what a very bad poem for the millennium was produced and broadcast by the Poet in Residence to the Dome. The quality of our language is vital to the quality of our world.

Chapter II of this book looked at language and languages. Chapter III considered poetry and time, particularly, poetry and *presence*. Part 1 of this chapter discussed how in the English radical tradition the de-supernaturalisation of God has gone hand in hand with the struggle for justice. It criticised Don Cupitt, who has written so well on religion as a human creation, for ignoring justice. It also looked at the two opposing uses that are made of the Christian story in Latin America.

This Part 2 picks up on earlier themes and focuses on the crux of the Christian story (a creation of the Poetic Genius), the Incarnation — embodiment — of the Word. As a preliminary to this, it will discuss the doctrine of the Trinity, which was developed side by side with that of the Incarnation, in an attempt to accommodate the paradox of an unchanging God becoming man. Then it will look briefly at the theology and liturgy — the Mass as the much-disputed 'real presence' — of Christ the Incarnate Word. We take this as just one example, from among many, of a religious story, simply because it is familiar and has had such tremendous resonance down the centuries. We assume throughout that both theology and liturgy are human creations. We look briefly at the furious debates by means of which fallible human in-fighters forged this theology. Then we consider what light these creations of 'God as Trinity' and 'God made Man' throw on 'the human form divine' — ourselves; and on poetry, which is itself 'incarnate word'.

The Jesus of the earliest — synoptic — gospels, Matthew, Mark and Luke, does not call himself God. Though he makes cryptic remarks like: 'No one knows the Son except the Father and no one knows the Father except the Son,'[100] his favourite term for himself is 'the Son of Man' — a reference to the book of Daniel. He proclaims the imminent coming of the reign of God on Earth — a reign of justice and peace, which is good news for the poor. In Mark, the earliest gospel, Jesus speaks of the Son of Man

---

[100] Matthew 11:27.

coming 'in the glory of his Father with the holy angels'[101] and promises: 'Truly, I tell you, there are some standing here who will not taste death until they see the kingdom of God come with power.'[102] He foretells the destruction of Jerusalem in AD 70 and that 'after that time of distress... then they will see the Son of Man coming in clouds with great power and glory.'[103] In the epilogue to the Gospel of John, Peter asks what will happen to John and Jesus answers:[104]

> 'If I want him to stay behind till I come, what does it matter to you?'... The rumour then went about among the brothers that this disciple would not die. Yet Jesus had not said to Peter, 'He will not die,' but 'If I want him to stay behind till I come.'

This sounds very like a survivor of John's apology for the fact that John *had* died and Jesus still had not come.

Paul told the early Christian community at Corinth: 'For as often as you eat this bread and drink the cup, you proclaim the Lord's death until he comes'[105] and they prayed: *'Marana tha!* Our Lord, come!'[106] But he did not come on clouds of glory and the longer they were disappointed the more believers were driven to do theology. We see this process beginning with the gospel of John (traditionally written in about the year AD 85 at the earliest, after the fall of Jerusalem), which is much more 'theological' than the earlier synoptic gospels. John's gospel begins with the proclamation of Jesus as God's Word *(Logos),* who actually is God: 'In the beginning was the Word and the Word was with

---

[101] Mark 8:38.
[102] Mark 9:1.
[103] Mark 13:26.
[104] John 21:21-3.
[105] 1 Corinthians 11:26.
[106] 1 Corinthians 16:22.

God and the Word was God.'[107] This same Word was the man Jesus whom people had known on Earth: 'The Word became flesh and lived among us, and we have seen his glory, the glory as of the Father's only Son, full of grace and truth.'[108]

For centuries Christian theologians struggled and feuded to develop a fuller statement of what these words involved, reaching an official agreement at Chalcedon in 451. With the conversion of the Emperor Constantine in 312, Christianity had become the religion of the Roman Empire. Constantine summoned the Council of Nicaea in 325, demanding an agreed statement from the contestants. He needed it for the peace of the Empire but of course he would not want any coming 'reign of God', which was good news for the poor, to subvert his own rule. Religious salvation was to be internal and fulfilment in another world. The statements of Nicaea and Chalcedon were theological definitions of the Church's now official position on the related doctrines of the Incarnation and the Trinity. Nevertheless, the earlier more political hopes of a coming utopia, a reign of justice and peace on Earth, in which the poor would be 'blessed', did not die out, and although theology was used as an oppressive ideology by the ruling powers, this same theology also interacted with the this-worldly utopian tradition and was used as a force or argument for liberation.

Here we can only note a few points in the fascinating story of the development of the doctrine of the Incarnation and Trinity from New Testament times up to Chalcedon, about which countless scholarly and polemical books have been written.[109] On Christ's

---

[107] John 1:1.
[108] John 1:14.
[109] For example, the classic, J.N.D. Kelly, *Early Christian Doctrines* (A & C Black, London 1958), from which some of the quotations in this chapter are taken.

pre-existence, the Apostolic Father, 'Barnabas'[110] and the second-century Apologist Justin both had the delightful idea that when at the creation God said: 'Let *us* make man...'[111] God the Father was talking to his Son, his Word. Irenaus[112] was an 'economic trinitarian', who held that the one God acted as a triad in the divine 'economy' or dispensation, that is, in creation, redemption and sanctification. The North African Tertullian,[113] the first theologian to use the term 'trinity', expressed how the Father's Word was 'a second in addition to himself' by comparing it to ourselves: *secundus quodammodo in te est sermo:* '[your] word is somehow a "second" in you.' The problem for Christian theologians was to define in what way one God could be three, and how Christ as a single individual could be both God and man.

Much of the fighting was caused by confusion of terms. In the Greek East the two distinguishing terms, *ousia* and *hypostasis*, were originally synonyms, meaning 'that which a thing is'. Gradually, *ousia* came to be used to mean 'substance' or 'essence' — what — and *hypostasis* to mean 'subsistent individual' — who — someone is. Different theologians expressed a whole range of positions about God and Christ. Modalism, for example, regarded Father, Son and Spirit as 'modes' of the godhead, whereas Arius[114] regarded the Son as inferior and not co-eternal with the Father and expressed this in his famous phrase 'there was when he was not'. Athanasius[115] opposed him and the Council of Nicaea in 325 defined the famous *homoousion:* that the Son was 'of the same

---

[110] 'Barnabas' wrote c.96-8.
[111] Genesis 1:26
[112] Irenaus c.140-202.
[113] Tertullian c. 160-220.
[114] Arius c. 280-336.
[115] Athanasius 295-373.

substance' as the Father. The historian Socrates[116] described the Council as:

> exactly like a battle by night, for both parties seemed to be in the dark about the grounds on which they were hurling abuse at each other. Those who objected to the word *homoousion* imagined that its adherents were bringing in the doctrine of Sabellius and Montanus [modalism]. So they called them blasphemers on the ground that they were undermining the personal subsistence of the Son of God. On the other hand, the protagonists of *homoousion* concluded that their opponents were introducing polytheism, and steered clear of them as importers of paganism.

Although the Council of Nicaea did not make clear that the phrase 'of the same substance' used in reference to God must mean the *one* single, indivisible divine substance, Athanasius took this point and he also extended it to the *homoousion* of the Spirit, defined at the Council of Constantinople in 381 as 'the Holy Spirit proceeding from the Father ['and the Son' was added later] who with the Father and the Son is likewise adored and glorified'.

The other two main terms used in the East were *physis* and *prosopon*. *Physis* was normally taken to mean 'nature' and used as equivalent to *ousia* ('substance'). *Prosopon* originally meant 'face', then was extended to mean 'the outward presentation of a person' and eventually, 'person' and used as equivalent to *hypostasis*. These confusing definitions caused fierce wrangling.

Cyril of Alexandria,[117] for example, used *physis* to mean 'concrete individual', which was why he said Christ had one *physis* (nature) and was attacked as a 'monophysite', because orthodoxy said that

---

[116] Socrates 380-c 450.
[117] Cyril of Alexandria died 444.

Christ had two natures, one divine and one human. For his part, Cyril thought Nestorius[118] held that Christ was two persons — God and man linked in some way — and managed to get him condemned. Probably, however, Nestorius was not a 'Nestorian'; when he said that Christ was two *hypostases* he was using *hypostasis* to mean 'nature'.

In the Latin West the main terms used were *persona* (person) for *prosopon* and *substantia* (substance) for *ousia*. Augustine, whose major work was his *De Trinitate*, developed the fertile idea that all three divine persons possess the same single divine substance or nature and what distinguishes them as three persons are their *subsistent relationships*, which will be discussed further below.

Finally, after centuries of polemic and political intrigue the Council of Chalcedon (today in Turkey) met in 451 and produced its definition:

> In agreement therefore with the holy fathers, we all unanimously teach that we should confess that our Lord Jesus Christ is one and *the same* Son, *the same* perfect in godhead and *the same* perfect in manhood, truly God and truly man, *the same* of a rational soul and body, consubstantial *(homoousion)* with the Father in godhead, and *the same* consubstantial *(homoousion)* with us in manhood, like us in all things except sin; begotten from the Father before the ages as regards his godhead, and in the last days, *the same*, for us and for our salvation begotten from the Virgin Mary, the mother of God *(theotokos)*, as regards his manhood; one and *the same* Christ, Son, Lord, only-begotten, made known in two natures, without confusion, without change, without division, without separation, the difference of the natures being by no means removed

---

[118] Nestorius died 451.

because of the union, but the property of each nature being preserved and coming together in one person *(prosopon/persona)* and one subsistence *(hypostasis/ subsistentia)* — not parted or divided into two persons *(prosopa/personae)*, but one and *the same* Son, only-begotten, divine Word, the Lord Jesus Christ, as the prophets of old and Jesus Christ himself have taught us about him and the creed of our fathers has handed down.

The vigorous prose of the Chalcedon definition with its ringing reiteration of *the same, the same, the same,* is very different from the way in which Jesus spoke about himself. John Hick's book *The Metaphor of God Incarnate*[119] argues convincingly that 'God incarnate' is a metaphor, because (apart from the fact that it does not tally with the gospel accounts of Jesus) no credible description can be given of how the Chalcedon definition of Christ's person could operate in practice.

Trinity and Incarnation *are* metaphors, but not for the reason Hick gives. Hick assumes that what he calls 'the Transcendent', the 'eternally Real', i.e. God, really exists and the Chalcedon account of this God becoming a human being — being both divine and human as one person — is figurative language. But it is this God himself or itself that is the metaphor. The Chalcedon definition cannot be taken literally because God cannot be taken literally. God is a creation of the human Poetic Genius, operating very forcefully in this magnificent prose poem.

Although the struggles that led up to Chalcedon took place a millennium and a half ago in a completely different world, this creation of the Poetic Genius and the metaphors of trinity and Incarnation have had an enormous effect and are worth exploring in this book's context of 'the poetry of Earth'.

---

[119] John Hick, *The Metaphor of God Incarnate* (SCM Press, London 1993).

One of the great struggles was for the *homoousion*, meaning 'consubstantial' or 'of the same substance'. It was because some of its opponents had produced the term *homoiousion*, meaning 'of similar substance' (rather than the same) that Gibbon sneered: the whole of Europe was in turmoil over an 'i'. Augustine in his *De Trinitate* had tried to work out how God could be three distinct persons — through their 'subsistent relationships' — each possessing the same whole divine nature. He had already reflected on this in his earlier work, his *Confessions:*

> The ultimate being exists in both simplicity and multiplicity, the Persons being defined by relation to each other, yet infinite in themselves. So the divine being is and knows itself and is immutably sufficient to itself because of the overflowing greatness of the unity.[120]

In Augustine's doctrine of the Trinity, God the infinite being is rational and knows himself completely, so completely that his self-knowledge or 'Word' is also infinite and therefore also God. Because God is all-knowing, God's self-knowledge is no less than God, the knower. Therefore this self-knowledge or Word is no less than personal. He is a distinct (but not separate) Person, the Second Person of the Trinity. The Second Person is called both 'Word', which indicates that it does not have a separate nature from the First Person (the knower or speaker), and 'Son', which indicates that he is a distinct Person from the First Person (the Father). Thus the Father possesses the whole, single divine nature *as Father* and the Son possesses it *as Son, as Word*. They are distinct persons through this relationship of father and son. It is through his Word that the First Person, Father, creates the world. In the opening words of John's gospel:

---

[120] Augustine, *Confessions*, translated by Henry Chadwick (Oxford World Classics, 1991), page 280.

In the beginning was the Word, and the Word was with God and the Word was God. He was in the beginning with God. All things were made through him...

As we have seen, the theology of the Spirit developed more slowly than that of the Word and the *homoousion* of the Spirit was not declared until the Council of Constantinople in 381, fifty-four years after Nicaea had declared the *homoousion* of the Word. One problem was how the 'procession' of the Spirit could differ from that of the Word, because, of course, the Father did not have two Sons. Again, it was Augustine who came up with the answer that the Spirit was a distinct 'subsistent relationship'. The Spirit was not 'begotten' but 'breathed' as the mutual love of the Father and Son — *'communem qua invicem se diligunt pater et filius caritatem'* — their love for one another, into which Father and Son pour everything they are, so it is also infinite, also a distinct Person. Augustine famously defined love as 'my love is my weight' [121] and thus the Spirit is the 'immutably sufficient' love by which the Father and Son 'gravitate' to one another.

As we noted earlier, in the picturesque language of Justin and 'Barnabas' when at creation God said: 'Let *us* make man...' he was talking to his Word. Both being and knowing are involved in creation: they are distinct but not separate. So is the Spirit who 'broods over the face of the waters'.

Indeed, we can look at the creator Trinity as a way of describing what creates us, what makes us what we are, what we are made of: that is, being, language and loving. We are, we exist. But from the moment we exist, we also become, so that we are what we are in relationship to others, through language and loving.

Augustine advises those who feel baffled to:

---

[121] *Confessions,* page 278.

Reflect upon the triad within their own selves... The three aspects I mean are being, knowing and willing *(esse, nosse and velle)*. For I am and I know and will. Knowing and willing I am. I know that I am and I will. I will to be and to know.[122]

The comparison Augustine invites us to make with our own selves is illuminating. The doctrine of the Trinity is a way of exploring being, knowing and loving (willing) within ourselves by creating a paradigm of infinite being, knowing and loving. For example, it is true that my word/words or knowledge/self-knowledge is distinct from myself but not separate. Unlike in the paradigmatic case of an infinite God, my knowledge/self-knowledge is not infinite — I do not know myself completely — so there is no question of it becoming a distinct person, equal to myself. Nevertheless it is both distinct but not separate from myself.

Like God, I can create a world through language, through my word/s. However, here the doctrine of the Trinity is a timely corrective to the postmodernist idea that a world we create is *nothing but* language. The world exists and is distinct from my knowledge of it, from my word/s. Likewise, I can create myself through language. As one version of the nursery rhyme goes: 'Twinkle, twinkle little star, what you speak is what you are.' But this is not the whole truth. I am not nothing but what I say about myself. Indeed, I can speak falsely. My being remains distinct (but not separate) from what I say about myself. As a poet, I might aspire to be like God in the Trinity and pour the whole of myself into my word/s. Because I am not infinite, I will never succeed. Nevertheless, one of the marks of a great poet is how much of him or her self has been poured into the work (even if the work is not in the least confessional). Obviously, we would not expect

---

[122] *Confessions*, page 279.

any poem to stand up and walk as a person distinct from the poet. But we do speak of poems 'having a life of their own'.

In the Trinity being 'begets' knowledge/self-knowledge and being and knowledge together 'breathe' love. We could regard this paradigm of infinite being as a poetic rendering both of evolution and the human self. In evolution 'being' evolves into rationality, we could say, 'begets' it. In the human self, being — energy which is 'eternal delight' — seeks knowledge and knowledge overflows into love. Obviously, our knowledge does not always overflow into love, but the paradigm of it doing so in infinite being makes sense. At our best, knowledge *does* overflow into love, will, action.

Two other terms used of the Trinity are 'circuminsession', that is, the three persons 'rest' or 'dwell' in one another and, changing just one letter, 'circumincession', that is, the three persons 'flow' into one another in an endless procession. In the finite human self, where being and the attainment of knowledge is gradual and limited, 'circumincession' means that when knowledge flows into love, love flows back into more being and so on round and round. The Trinity then becomes a paradigm not just of the growth of the individual human self but of the human species as a whole towards a desired fullness or utopia.

The paradoxical idea that there are *relationships* in the one divine Being suggests that the human self requires *other persons* for completeness. Each human being is a *separate* person with our own *separate* human nature, which we only share generically with our fellow humans. But the paradigm of the Trinity suggests that in order to develop fully we need relationships, we need other people. It also suggests a completeness, a fullness, which we could only attain if the whole human race was involved in gradually increasing being, knowledge and love towards a better society. Of course, as humans we can never attain perfection or infinity, but the construct of the Trinity posits being, knowledge and love as the three relationships through which humanity can increase towards an ideal, both individually and socio-politically.

Traditional Christian theology would, of course, put this the other way round. Assuming that God, the Trinity, is real, it would describe the salvation of humanity as a process of becoming godlike, or even of deification — *theosis*. The way this salvation is to be achieved is through the Incarnation of the Word. In the classic formula: 'God became man, so that man might become God.' Man means both each human individual (including — somewhat reluctantly on the part of some theologians! — women) and the human race as a whole, humanity.

The Trinity is a very rich and illuminating poetic construct of the supreme being. But it is just one construct. Although most religions have a supreme being, they construct it differently. Although Christian orthodoxy insists that God has no sex, we note that the terms used for the theology of the Trinity are relentlessly masculine: Father, Son, he. The feminine is conspicuously absent. Perhaps, that was why the struggle to describe Mary by the term *theotokos* (mother of God or God-bearer: first defined at the Council of Ephesus in 431, repeated at Chalcedon, 451) assumed such importance. Nestorius was condemned partly because he was so violently opposed to it. Although, of course, this did not make Mary a goddess, it did offer Christians a female to include in their cult. The common Catholic name for Mary is Our Lady.

The poet Ernesto Cardenal is a Catholic priest but highly unorthodox on the Trinity. In his poem 'Quetzalcóatl' (and elsewhere), instead of the normal masculine Spanish word for 'Spirit': *Espíritu* he invents a feminine form: *Espírita*, so that God the Father and God the (female) Spirit become the divine pair who generate the Son:

Como en el cristianismo:
Dios Padre y Dios Espírita.
¿Y el Hijo?
El hombre.

As in Christianity:
God the Father and God the Spiritess.
And the Son?
Man.

Just before this he has said of Quetzalcóatl:

He was the God of Tolan
creator of pulque and maize.
The God of Tolan, 'heart of the people.'
He is the same Ometéotl
(Ome = Two, Téotl = God),
the Holy Pair.
From whence children are sprinkled onto the Earth.

Another name for this creator god was Ometecutli-Omecíhuatl, the Lord and Lady of Duality. As a Catholic priest, Cardenal clearly suggests that the ancient Mexican story of the creator god as male and female offers an element lacking in the traditional version of the Christian story of the Trinity.

The refrain of the definition of Chalcedon is 'the same':

Our Lord Jesus Christ is one and *the same* Son, *the same* perfect in godhead and *the same* perfect in manhood, truly God and truly man, *the same* of a rational soul and body, consubstantial *(homoousion)* with the Father in godhead, and *the same* consubstantial *(homoousion)* with us in manhood...

This is the mystery of the Incarnation: that it was *the same* divine Word, Second Person of the Trinity who became a human being with a human mother, Mary. The same person who fully possesses the same divine nature as the Father *(homoousios* in godhead) became a human being *(homoousios* with us). As the infinite divine nature is indivisible, *homoousios* in godhead means wholly possessing the one single divine nature. But human nature means both the characteristics possessed by the whole human species (generic) and the particular human nature possessed by each human individual. So *homoousios* with us means that Christ both shares our single generic human nature with all the rest of the species, and has his own particular human nature as one human among many. He was born into a particular culture, in a particular time and place.

It was the Second Person, the Word, who became incarnate. Aquinas thought there was no reason why the Father or Spirit should not have become incarnate themselves but that it was more *appropriate* that it should be the Son, the Word. This was because one of the purposes of the Incarnation was to reveal God, so that we could come to know him. The Second Person, the Word, subsists as God's own self-knowledge. As the prologue to John's gospel puts it: [124]

> The Word became flesh and lived among us, and we have seen his glory, the glory of the Father's only Son, full of grace and truth... No one has ever seen God. It is God the only Son, who is close to the Father's heart, who has *made him known.*

The Chalcedon statement says he came into the world for us and for our salvation. Knowing God is part of this salvation but salvation means more than that. In his prologue John says: 'to all

---

[124] John 1: 14, 18.

who received him, who believed in his name, he gave power to become children of God.'[125] Thus, although Christ was the 'only-begotten Son' the rest of us could become God's sons and daughters *in* Christ.

As Paul puts it in his letter to the Ephesians: 'He [God] destined us for adoption as his children through Jesus Christ.'[126] Paul develops this idea through his theory of 'recapitulation' *(anakephalaiosis)*. It was God's plan 'for the fullness of time to gather up [recapitulate: *anakephalaiosasthai*] all things in him, things in heaven and things on Earth.' Through the birth, death and resurrection of Christ, not only is humanity forgiven but 'adopted', 'gathered up', 'recapitulated' in Christ and therefore in God.

Irenaus[127] developed this idea of recapitulation in the succinct formula: 'He became what we are (human) in order to enable us to become what he is (God).' We became estranged from God through our solidarity with Adam and reconciled with God through our solidarity with Christ, 'the second Adam', who has 'recapitulated' the whole human race. But the suggestion is that we have not just become 'reconciled' with God. Because Christ is both God and man, in him humanity as a whole and each human individual can 'become' God. As Athanasius[128] later expressed it, humans:

> could not become sons [of God], being by nature creatures, otherwise than by receiving the Spirit of the natural and true Son. Wherefore, that this might be, 'the Word became flesh' that he might make man capable of godhead.

---

[125] John 1:12.
[126] Ephesians 1:5.
[127] Irenaus c.140-202.
[128] Athanasius 295-373.

Or again: 'He indeed assumed humanity that we might become God.'[129] This concept of deification *(theosis)* was more prominent in the East than the West.

There were endless debates about the way in which salvation, or redemption as it was also called, happened. Augustine's famous phrase was *felix culpa* — 'lucky sin' (of Adam) — because he thought that if Adam had not fallen, there would have been no Incarnation. On the other hand, one of the reasons why Hopkins so loved the medieval Oxford theologian, Duns Scotus, was that Scotus taught that the Incarnation would have happened anyway.

As with the Trinity, an atheist can look at the story of the Incarnation the other way round. It is a story of God becoming human. If we assume that God is a human creation, we can see it as a story of humanity bringing the divine being it created and set in heaven above *down to Earth,* restoring God to humanity.

If God is a creation of the human Poetic Genius, then we can create both good and evil gods. Good and evil both exist in humanity and the gods we create are extrapolations of human potential, perhaps to the infinite. So, as we saw in Part 1 of this chapter, Blake has two 'Divine Image' poems, in one of which the 'human form divine' is 'love, mercy, pity, peace'; and in the other, 'cruelty has a human heart... terror the human form divine'.

However, gods may be more than just extrapolations of human potential; they may ontologise other *cosmic* forces as well. For example, the Christian God the Father is the creator of the cosmos. He ontologises, that is, he is the 'isness' of the forces that create the cosmos. When theologians talk about human beings becoming God through the Incarnation of the Word, they

---

[129] Quoted in J.N.D. Kelly, *Early Christian Doctrines,* page 130.

do not mean that human beings will become — though they may encapsulate — all the forces that create the cosmos.

In the Christian God, Being, Word and Love are three distinct persons. For human beings 'becoming God' can only mean growing in knowledge and love towards an ideal perfection (impossible to attain fully) and sharing in the being and power that created the cosmos in a way appropriate to humanity. 'Becoming God' in this sense is also a way of saying that human growth in knowledge and power must be consistent with love or, to put it another way, must be used for loving ends.

The monotheistic insight in the creation of one *single* ultimate divine being is that God is universal, and not a tribal God, not for one human group against another. The insight in the creation of this God as *trinity* is that power and being are related to knowledge and love. They are distinct but not separate. This sets up a human ideal where being more and knowing more are related to and constrained by loving more. The contrary god, Blake's Nobodaddy, the god of cruelty, jealousy, terror and secrecy, is declared to be an idol, that demands and feeds on death.

Because humanity has the potential for evil as well as for good, the Christian theology of salvation through the Incarnation of the Word is twofold. On the one hand, there is the theology of salvation as *theosis* — becoming God (or 'children of God'). On the other hand, there is the theology of salvation as *redemption* or *ransom* for our sins through the death and resurrection of Jesus. These two strands have existed in all kinds of combinations and the ransom theory has been expressed in picturesque and sometimes bizarre ways. Sometimes the debt is paid to the devil, who has obtained some claim over humanity, rather as one redeems something from a pawn shop. Sometimes it is paid to God the Father, as a kind of indemnity for the affront to his majesty caused by human sin. For example, in the glorious 'Harrowing of Hell' in *Piers Plowman*,[130] Jesus tricks the devil by becoming man and disguising his godhead, so that he manages to release 'his own [people]' from the devil's power in hell. Though vivid, some of these ransom scenarios are, to put it mildly, theologically problematic.

But the serious point being made is that there are obstacles to *theosis*, to human transformation into divine goodness. Human beings are not all good. They can be cruel, jealous, greedy and terrifying. The salvation of humanity is a struggle. Jesus does not commit suicide as a sacrificial offering. He is crucified by 'the sin of the world'. Cruelty and terror win the first round. But then he is raised from the dead, he 'conquers sin'. The story of the resurrection is an affirmation that though the powers of evil are strong, the powers of life and goodness are even stronger. It affirms that, because human beings do evil as well as good, salvation is not just an intellectual process, a *gnosis* that will make us divine. As in the Trinity, human salvation requires that power and knowledge flow into, 'breathe', love, goodwill, good action, which will probably involve conflict and suffering.

The story of Christ's passion is a paradigm of this struggle. This is how Paul describes it to the Philippians in the words of what was probably a baptismal hymn:[131]

> Though he was in the form of God, [he] did not regard equality with God as something to be exploited, but emptied himself *(eskenosen)*, taking the form of a slave, being born in human likeness. And being found in human form, he humbled himself and became obedient to the point of death — even death on a cross. Therefore God also highly exalted him and gave him the name that is

---

[130] *Piers Plowman*, Passus 18. A quatrain from it is quoted on page 94.
[131] Philippians 1:6-11.

above every name, so that at the name of Jesus every knee should bend in heaven and on Earth and under the Earth, and every tongue should confess that Jesus Christ is Lord to the glory of God the Father.

Thus the Incarnation of the Word involves an engagement with the world, a *kenosis* — self-emptying — into the world, a struggle that may be to the death. The story of the resurrection affirms that the divine Word, the power of love, is not finally defeated. That is why in speaking of God's 'plan for the fullness of time to recapitulate all things Christ,' Paul says, 'In him we have redemption through his blood.'[132] *Theosis* occurs through Christ's death and resurrection.

Nevertheless, Christ goes away and the salvation of the world has visibly not yet happened. He sends the Spirit (Love, Will, in the theology of the Trinity) to his disciples to help them complete his work. Now that Jesus has gone away, Paul develops the idea of the Church as Christ's body,[133] with Christ as the head and others in the Church having different functions and different gifts 'to equip the saints for the work of... building up the body Christ.' In his *Letter to the Colossians*[134] Paul also says that his own sufferings are 'filling up what is lacking in Christ's sufferings for the sake of his body, that is, the church.' In other words, human effort is also required.

Jesus preached the coming of the reign of God, a state of justice and peace which would be good news for the poor. This kingdom has not come. It is a metaphor for the creation of a just society on Earth, which we know will not be inaugurated by the Son of Man coming on clouds of glory, but, if it comes at all, by human struggle.

---

[132] Ephesians 1:6.
[133] Ephesians 4:4.
[134] Colossians 1:24.

We saw how the delay in the coming of the reign of God caused Christians to turn to theology with the resulting development of the doctrines of the Trinity and Incarnation reaching a high point at Chalcedon. In one way, this was a *relegation* of the salvation preached by Christ, inward to the soul and upward to another world. In other words, salvation was de-politicised and attention was turned away from the gospel as good news for the poor *soon, in this world*. Nevertheless, the developing theology of the Trinity, Incarnation and redemption, *interacts* with the this-worldly utopian tradition and can be used as a force or argument for liberation. The struggle continues for control of the Word.

This has happened throughout Christian history. We have already discussed two examples First, in the English Revolution Gerrard Winstanley spoke of 'Christ rising again in the sons and daughters', which he connected with poor people having enough land to till and support themselves on. Secondly in our own time, liberation theology identifies Christ on Earth today with 'the crucified people' — the poor and dispossessed — and their struggle to rise with Christ's resurrection.

Thus Jesus' own metaphor of the imminent reign of God, which will be good news for the poor is one metaphor for a state of justice on Earth that humans have to struggle for. The theology of the Trinity and Incarnation (including the death and resurrection of the Word) can be interpreted as a parallel metaphor for this same human salvation, which again will not come by divine intervention but is a human project and must be here on Earth or nowhere. The simple message of the imminent reign of God, good news for the poor, was marginalised — even 'killed off' — as subversive, and a highly complex theology developed to describe the saving spiritual transformation made available to us by Christ, the God-Man.

However, the original, subversive gospel message of justice on Earth keeps managing to resurrect itself in the very theology that attempted to relegate it. Attempts to keep the poor in their place (which started, of course, in this story, with the Roman and priestly authorities killing Jesus himself) have constantly been answered with a fightback, in which they rise again. Jesus of Nazareth existed in history. It appears he mistakenly preached the imminent reign of God, to be inaugurated by himself, the Son of Man, coming on clouds of glory. This did not happen but the myth of the imminent reign of God and the myth of divine Incarnation constructed round Jesus — God becoming man for man to become God — interweave as metaphors. As political action and as changing of mind and attitude *(metanoia)*, they become warp and woof of a whole — unfinished — historical tapestry of an ongoing human struggle.

The kingdom is taking a long time to come, because of what is lacking: justice and peace on Earth. The central message of the Sermon on the Mount is: Seek first the kingdom and its justice — τὴν βασιλείαν καὶ τὴν δικαιοσύνην αὐτοῦ — and all these things shall be yours as well.'[135] Paul says of Christ:[136]

> When he ascended on high he led captivity captive; he gave gifts to his people. When it says, 'He ascended', what does it mean but that he had also descended into the lower parts of the Earth? He who descended is the same one who ascended far above all the heavens, so that he might fill all things.

The story of Christ ascending into heaven as glorified humanity to 'fill all things' is prefigurative of the fulfilment of humanity, when it reaches 'maturity... the measure of the stature of the

---

[135] Or: 'Seek first [God's] kingdom and his justice': Matthew 6:33.
[136] Ephesians 4:7.

fullness of Christ',[136] that is, when the kingdom comes and justice and peace reign on Earth.

Meanwhile, until it comes, Christ's social body (a metaphor for potentially fulfilled and glorified humanity, when the 'new Jerusalem' is brought down from heaven to Earth) coheres and grows through *liturgy*, that is, its social poetry. Together the community goes through a yearly cycle of the seasons, with which the life, death and resurrection of Christ is symbolically connected (birth at the winter solstice, death and resurrection in spring) and other special events and persons are commemorated on special days.

Liturgy is poetic language intended to be *performative*. Obviously, it can perform some things (e.g. create a sense of community) but not others (e.g. bring an end to a famine-causing drought). The heart of the liturgy is the Eucharist. This is how Paul describes it to the Corinthians:[137]

> For I received from the Lord what I also handed on to you, that the Lord Jesus on the night when he was betrayed took a loaf of bread, and when he had given thanks, he broke it and said, 'This is my body that is broken for you. Do this in remembrance of me.' In the same way he took the cup also, after supper, saying, 'This cup is the new covenant in my blood. Do this, as often as you drink it, in remembrance of me.' For as often as you eat this bread and drink the cup, you proclaim the Lord's death *until he comes*.

Thus the Eucharist looks forward to the Lord's coming, the reign of justice and peace on Earth. And it looks back to remember his death. In chapter III we discussed poetry as *wording presence*. The liturgy of the Eucharist is social poetry, which commemorates the

---

[136] Ephesians 4:13.
[137] 1 Corinthians 11:16.

Lord's passion and resurrection with bread and wine and thereby summons his *presence*. Of course, throughout Church history, there have been passionate, indeed murderous, debates about the mode of this presence, the meaning of 'real presence'. It is said that before she became Queen Elizabeth I, while her Catholic sister Mary was on the throne, Elizabeth invented her equivocal quatrain to save herself from being burnt alive:

His was the word that spake it
He took the bread and brake it
And what his word doth make it
I do believe and take it.

In the Eucharist Christ's presence is summoned by repeating the words: 'This is my body' and 'this is my blood' over the bread and wine. The words are *performative:* Christ becomes present to the gathered community in the (symbols, concrete metaphors, of) bread and wine. As well as this, the *ceremony itself* is performative. It articulates the community gathered together as a body, the (still not fully 'mature') social body of Christ. Physically, and here symbolically, 'we are what we eat'.

In the Preface to the Canon of the Mass, during which the bread and wine are consecrated with special words, as well as the particular feast (such as Christmas or Easter), saints and martyrs, particularly from the early Church, are called to mind and in this way also made present. The definition of a sacrament is that it effects what it signifies. The Eucharist *signifies* and *effects* the presence of Christ, in the bread and wine, in the partaking community present at the Mass, and as the presence of the historical body of Christ in great figures from Church history. This Church history is then carried forward in the Mass that is taking place. The Eucharist is a social poem of commemoration, consolidation and prefigurative politics.

If we think of poetry as *wording presence*, the social poetry of the Eucharist *presents* Christ's past death and resurrection. It makes them present. It also *presents*, by anticipation, Christ's body's future 'stature' — 'the measure of the stature of the fullness of Christ' — the 'realised eschatology' of the 'human form divine', when the kingdom comes and justice reigns on Earth. That is why the Eucharist is repeated 'until he comes'. Meanwhile, the poetic words and symbolic actions of the ceremony enthuse (= 'en-god') the participants, so that performative becomes prefigurative, that is, the 'now' symbolises and anticipates the 'not yet'.

Different communities have developed different liturgies of the Eucharist. Here we look at just one example, the Nicaraguan *Misa campesina* or 'Peasant Mass'. Earlier this chapter we discussed the liberation theologian Jon Sobrino's view that the 'reign of God' means justice on Earth, especially for 'the crucified people', which is where Christ is to be found on Earth today:

> It is the crucified people who make Christ's passion *present today*, those who fill up in their bodies what is lacking in Christ's passion. They are Christ's crucified body in history.

Like Jesus, they are crucified by the 'sin of the world', the 'structural sin' of the powers that rule the world which inflicts poverty, suffering and death upon them. In their hope and their struggle for life they are 'rising again'. This is the theological background to the *Misa campesina*, which translates the traditional phases of the Roman Mass into these terms. For example, the closing sections of the Nicene-Constantinople creed of the Roman Mass affirm faith in Christ's resurrection and what follows from it:

> And the third day he rose again according to the Scriptures: and ascended into heaven. He sits at the right hand of the

Father: and he will come again with glory to judge the living and the dead: and his kingdom shall have no end... I await the resurrection of the dead and the life of the world to come.

When the *Misa campesina* was sung in a church in London in 1986, the popular Catholic weekly, *The Universe,* had a shock-horror banner headline: COMRADE CHRIST! This was because of its translation of the creed:

I trust in you, comrade,
human Christ, Christ the worker,
death you've overcome.
Your fearful suffering
forged the new human being
formed for freedom.

You are rising again
in every arm that's raised
to defend the people
from being exploited and kept down,
because you're living on the farm,
in the factory and in school.
I believe in your unstinting struggle.
I believe in your resurrection.

Yo creo en vos, compañero,
Cristo humano, Cristo obrero,
de a la muerte vencedor.
Con tu sacrificio inmenso
engendraste al hombre nuevo
para la liberación.

Vos estás resucitando
en cada brazo que se alza

para defender al pueblo
del dominio explotador,
porque estás vivo en el rancho,
en la fábrica, en la escuela;
creo en tu lucha sin tregua,
creo en tu resurrección.[138]

This is a translation or incarnation of the traditional creed into a particular context. Christ has 'overcome death'. His suffering has 'forged the new human being formed for freedom'. Christ's body is still on Earth in his community, which through the Spirit, is struggling also to 'rise again', so that the 'reign of God', of justice, will be realised on Earth. The theology of salvation or liberation, as it is usually called in Latin America, sees Christ's death and resurrection as inaugural and paradigmatic. It regards the current struggles of his body on Earth today as 'filling up what is wanting in the sufferings of Christ', 'rising again' to complete the task of bringing the reign of justice on Earth. The passion is still going on and the resurrection is also a process.

In the *Misa campesina* the story of Christ's death and resurrection becomes a metaphor or poem of the current, messy, ongoing political struggles for justice. When it expresses faith that Christ has 'overcome death', it is not affirming that dead people will rise from the dead, but that in a just world people will not starve to death or be massacred and their lives cut short. It does not affirm that the final 'reign of God' will be brought to Earth by Christ returning on clouds of glory, but expresses faith that through struggle to 'defend the people' justice will finally come. The

---

[138] *Nicaraguan Peasant Mass (Misa campesina),* Carlos Mejía Godoy, 10 songs, reprinted with new introduction by Dinah Livingstone (Nicaragua Solidarity Campaign, London 1996). The Mass was sung in Spanish with parts in English at St Aloysius, Somers Town, London, on Low Sunday 1986. The translation given here is closer to the original than in the published version, in which some lines had to be singable in English.

vehicle of the paradigm or metaphor — Christ's death and resurrection — adds strength to its tenor — the struggle for justice on Earth — rather than distracting or sidelining it with the illusion of a supernatural afterlife.

We have discussed liturgy as poetry, but what about the other way round? We no longer live in a predominantly Christian culture. Do atheists or humanists need or want liturgy, that is, social poetry, to mark the turning year, major life events, to commemorate a history and articulate hopes and fears for the present and future? In such a fragmented society, is such a liturgy even possible? Even if it is not, it still remains a challenge to poets in a secular age to produce poetry with as broad a scope as the poetry of the past, embracing all human experience, political and mystical aspirations, and all the gods and demons that 'reside in the human breast'.

CHAPTER V
MORE THINGS IN HEAVEN AND EARTH

What is the scope of poetry? The answer can only be all human experience and if, as Blake maintains, religions are creations of the Poetic Genius, then this includes religious experience. Religion comes within the scope of poetry not just as part of human experience, but because as well as having political power (with an economic base) for good or ill, it has poetic power and vice versa, poetry has power that can be described as religious. What is this power?

In his lecture on the 'Theory and Function of the *Duende*'[139] García Lorca says:

> The *duende* is a power and not a behaviour, it is a struggle and not a concept... This "mysterious power that everyone feels but that no philosopher has explained" is in fact the spirit of the Earth.

Later in the lecture he expands this:

> The appearance of the *duende* always presupposes a radical change of all forms based on old structures. It gives a sensation of freshness wholly unknown, having a quality of newly-created rose, of miracle, and produces in the end an almost religious enthusiasm. In all Arabic music, dance or

---

[139] 'Theory and Function of the *Duende*', lecture reprinted in Lorca: *Selected Poems*, translated by J.L. Gili (Penguin, 1960).

song, the appearance of the *duende* is greeted with vociferous shouts of *Alá! Alá!:* 'God! God!'

Of course, not all poems are greeted with vociferous shouts of 'God! God!' The scope of poetry includes not just the heights and depths of human experience, but also ordinary everyday things, which may, for example, be funny, embarrassing or muddling. But we don't have to allow a fashionable cult of the mundane and domestic in English poetry to enforce the exclusion of either political poetry, or poetry concerned with ideas and the wider reaches of human experience. If religion is a poetic creation, natural rather than supernatural, then even for atheists the scope of poetry must be broad enough to embrace religious experience as part of human experience.

Despite describing their experiences as unutterable, most mystics have been writers, often poets. Poets and mystics may or may not belong to a particular religious community and speak in that particular language (when they do belong they usually get into trouble with the authorities). Mainstream Christian theology, for example, holds that God, the Infinite Being, is not part of the universe he created. In that sense, he is 'outside' it, though at the same time he is 'everywhere'. But mystics, including Christian mystics, often describe a union with Being, in which the distinction between 'outside' and 'inside' dissolves.

For atheists, who do not believe in a supernatural god, there is no 'outside' the universe, but this has not prevented atheists from becoming mystics; plenty of mystics in various traditions have been atheists (and many mystics in theistic traditions have been called atheists) because the experience they describe of blissful union with Being appears to be the same, whether they believe in a supernatural god or not. This means a supernatural god is not necessary to mystical experience. Mystical experience is akin to poetic experience.

Chapter III reflected on poetry and presence. Chapter IV discussed religion as a creation of the Poetic Genius. This chapter V will expand on both of these themes. It will consider 'more things in heaven and Earth', on the grounds that enormously rich and poetic religious traditions should not be jettisoned just because they have been de-supernaturalised, that is, brought down to Earth. The chapter will be in two parts. Part 1, 'The Deep Power of Joy' will look briefly at some poems by four different poets, three English and one Spanish.

1
THE DEEP POWER OF JOY

In his 'Lines written a few miles above Tintern Abbey',[141] which he revisited with his sister Dorothy in July 1798, Wordsworth describes the 'tranquil restoration' brought to him 'mid the din of towns and cities' by the memory of nature's 'forms of beauty' and then goes on to speak of what else nature has given him:

> ...Another gift
> Of aspect more sublime; that blessed mood,
> In which the burthen of the mystery,
> In which the heavy and the weary weight
> Of all this unintelligible world
> Is lightened: — that serene and blessed mood,
> In which the affections gently lead us on,
> Until, the breath of this corporeal frame,
> And even the motion of our human blood
> Almost suspended, we are laid asleep
> In body, and become a living soul:
> While with an eye made quiet by the power
> Of harmony, and the deep power of joy,
> We see into the life of things.

In this trance-like state it is beauty, 'the power of harmony', that quietens the eye and it is the 'deep power of joy' that enables the poet to see into the life of things. Later in the poem he says that now he has passed his 'thoughtless youth', he has often heard 'the still sad music of humanity' and with it:

---

[141] First published 1798. Quotations from Wordsworth's poetry in this chapter are taken from *Wordsworth: Poetry and Prose*, ed. David Nichol Smith (Oxford University Press, 1921).

> ...I have felt
> A presence that disturbs me with the joy
> Of elevated thoughts; a sense sublime
> Of something far more deeply interfused,
> Whose dwelling is the light of setting suns,
> And the round ocean, and the living air,
> And the blue sky, and in the mind of man,
> A motion and a spirit, that impels
> All thinking things, all objects of all thought,
> And rolls through all things.

This presence is not a person; it is 'something far more deeply interfused' — Being itself, Nature itself? This cosmic union with a single 'motion and a spirit that impels' and 'rolls through all things', this sense of an unnamed presence, apprehended vaguely as something interfused is one strand of mystical experience described again and again in many cultures and many poetries. The second strand of mystical experience, which often interweaves with the first to form a 'double helix', is the erotic.

In his 'Ode: Intimations of Immortality' Wordsworth describes how 'the things which I have seen I now can see no more'. The 'glory and the freshness' have passed: 'there hath passed away a glory from the Earth'.

> Heaven lies about us in our infancy!
> Shades of the prison house begin to close
> Upon the growing boy...
> At length the Man perceives it die away
> And fade into the light of common day.

Wordworth's ecstasy, the deep wellspring of his poetry, comes from the passionate communion with nature he first experienced in childhood. This *Ode* was begun in March 1802 (completed in March 1804), and he married Mary Hutchinson in October 1802.

It seems the marriage was very happy and even many years later they wrote astonishingly passionate love letters to each other. The beautiful poem 'She was a Phantom of Delight' (1803-4) describes Mary but Wordsworth's mystical poetry does not contain the erotic component of a sense of self-lack needing someone else, at the risk of being 'lost' or 'transformed' in the other, a human person who is not me. Possibly this was because as well as being 'a spirit still and bright/With something of an angel light' Mary was his bread-and-butter, day-to-day contentment:

> A Creature not too bright or good
> For human nature's daily food.

Possibly, it was because Wordsworth's poetic gift could be described in Keats' ambivalent phrase as the 'egotistical sublime'. He addresses nature: 'Oh ye Fountains, Meadows, Hills, and Groves,/Think not of any severing of our loves!' This is an I-it relationship: 'it' can't answer back. He is the great English poet of 'cosmic union' with nature, experienced as a form of self-enhancement, but it is intriguing to wonder whether 'the glory and the dream' faded because his mysticism was single-stranded and lacked the twin strand of erotic self-loss in the other: so a 'single helix' was unsustainable.

The *Ode* is a poem of loss — of the 'visionary gleam'. Nevertheless, in a common pattern for Wordsworth, the poem describes a loss that is not total loss; gain is derived from it. Firstly:

> ...those obstinate questionings
> Of sense and outward things,
> Fallings from us, vanishings;
> Blank misgivings of a Creature
> Moving about in worlds not realised.

Secondly, a greater awareness of the human heart:

> Thanks to the human heart by which we live,
> Thanks to its tenderness, its joys, and fears,
> To me the meanest flower that blows can give
> Thoughts that do often lie too deep for tears.

Coleridge[141] finished his 'Letter to Sara Hutchinson' on April 4th 1802 and the poem is partly a dialogue with Wordsworth's *Ode*, begun in that same spring of 1802 and finished two years later. Coleridge published a cut version of his poem addressed to Wordsworth as 'Edmund' with the title 'Dejection: An Ode' in the *Morning Post* on Wordworth's wedding day, 4th October 1802.

Coleridge's poem expresses a much more terrible sense of lack and loss, which inanimate nature cannot console. He beautifully describes the natural beauties he can see, where he is living in the Lake District:

> I see them all, so excellently fair!
> I see, not feel how beautiful they are.

His urgent confessional poem is addressed to Sara Hutchinson and because he is denied the warmth and fulfilment of loving and being loved, he has lost the power of joy and with it his creative power.

> O Sara! We receive but what we give,
> And in *our* life alone does Nature live.
> Our's is her Wedding Garment, our's her Shroud —
> And would we aught behold of higher Worth
> Than that inanimate cold World allow'd

---

[141] Quotations from Coleridge's poems in this chapter are taken from *Coleridge Poems*, ed. John Beer (Everyman edition, J.M. Dent, London 1974).

> To the poor loveless ever anxious Crowd,
> Ah! From the Soul itself must issue forth
> A Light, a Glory, and a luminous Cloud
> Enveloping the Earth.

This 'beautiful and beauty-making power' is Joy: 'Joy, Sara! is the Spirit and the Power.' There was a time for Coleridge when 'the joy within me dallied with Distress' and 'Hope grew round me like the climbing Vine'.

> But now Ill Tidings bow me down to Earth —
> Nor care I, that they rob me of my Mirth —
> But oh! Each visitation
> Suspends what Nature gave me at my Birth
> My shaping spirit of Imagination.

Nature alone cannot comfort him. He needs happiness in human I-you relationships. Because of his children he is trapped in an unhappy marriage:

> My own peculiar Lot, my house-hold Life
> It is, it will remain, Indifference or strife.

He is excluded from the close happy circle, the 'significant group' of 'Mary and William and dear Dorothy' and he cannot have Sara. He would not wish to be 'a withered branch upon a blossoming tree.' But even if Sara is not happy herself, he must still renounce her:

> But O! to mourn for thee, and to forsake
> All power, all hope of giving comfort to thee —
> To know that thou art weak and worn with pain
> And not to hear thee, Sara! Not to view thee —
> Not to sit beside thy Bed
> Not to press thy aching Head,

> Not to bring thee Health again —
> At least to hope, to try…

He is tormented by memory of a lost magical evening:

> When Mary, thou and I together were
> The low decaying Fire our only light…
> Dear Mary! On her Lap my head she lay'd
> Her hand was on my Brow
> Even as my own is now;
> And on my Cheek I felt thy eye-lash play.
> Such Joy I had…

At the end of the poem he does not address 'ye Fountains, Meadows, Hills, and Groves'. In his overwhelming need for human warmth and tenderness, he addresses Sara:

> Sister and Friend of my devoutest Choice!
> Thou being innocent and full of love
> And nested with the Darlings of thy Love
> And feeling in thy Soul, Heart, Lips, and Arms
> Even what the conjugal and mother Dove
> That borrows genial Warmth from those she warms,
> Feels in her thrill'd wings, blessedly outspread…

This blissful warmth is mutual, the mother dove is warmed by those she warms. Her warmth is motherly but also 'conjugal'. Coleridge feels he cannot do without it and he has lost it, and with it his power of poetry. He has lost his spirit. Coleridge was well aware that the dove was the usual image for the Holy Spirit, who at the creation when the Earth was 'formless and empty' (*tohu* and *bohu*), 'brooded over the face of the waters.' Sara, who is absent, whom he has lost, is a sort of goddess to him, embodying the spirit of Joy, necessary to his creative power. In his anguish he listens to the wind:

>...What a scream
> Of agony by torture lengthen'd out
> That Lute sent forth!

His pain recalls Psalm 22, whose first line Jesus quoted on the cross: 'My God, my God, why hast thou forsaken me?'

> I am poured out like water,
> and my bones are out of joint;
> my heart is like wax,
> it is melted within my breast;
> my strength is dried up like a potsherd,
> and my tongue cleaves to my jaws;
> thou dost lay me in the dust of death.

In the poem he seems to assume that Sara does love him in return but they have renounced this love. Her feelings are unclear. Four years later on 27th December 1806, Coleridge was tortured by seeing (or imagining he saw) Wordsworth and Sara in bed together with 'her beautiful breasts displayed'. In March 1810, after many months of helping Coleridge night after night with the production of his journal *The Friend,* Sara had had enough and decided to leave the Wordsworth household and go and live with her brother Tom in Wales. Coleridge was devastated. *The Friend* ceased publication and Coleridge knew he was no longer welcome at the Wordsworths, either.

Wordsworth took his loving and sustaining household for granted. He lost his 'visionary gleam' because it came from a sense of impersonal mystical communion with nature that faded as he grew older. His loving relationships with other people were not of a kind to inspire him to mystical poetry. Coleridge's complaint in his 'Letter to Sara Hutchinson' that his loss of joy has led to the loss of his 'shaping Spirit of Imagination' is actually contradicted by the poem itself. In both its forms, it remains one of his greatest poems. The 'Letter' version brilliantly communicates loneliness as the sense of loss of vital force, both animal and spiritual. His loss of Sara, his lack of a loving household, makes him realise that giving and receiving warmth from other people is even more vital to him — his self and his poetry — than the most beautiful natural objects. Joy, whose essential nurturer is human warmth, is the power of poetry. Without it 'a wise passiveness' will not work. In the dialectic that his poem describes between the inner state of mind and feeling and the outside world, the former predominates:

Joy, Sara! Is the Spirit and the Power
That wedding nature to us gives in Dower
A new Earth and a new Heaven.

Although this is one of his most magnificent poems, Coleridge is right that his loss of joy led to the decline of his poetry. Wordsworth and Coleridge gave us some of the most potent poems in the language, which even two hundred years later have 'passed into the fabric of the mind' of so many speakers of English. If both poets declined, it was for different reasons — Wordsworth from a certain one-strandedness or rigidity, Coleridge who saw both sides, as well as all the millions of variations, saw them from a position of absence, distance, lack, loss.

When as a Jesuit Hopkins[142] was miserably sent to work at St Aloysius in Oxford, a city he had greatly loved, he wrote to his friend Robert Bridges:

---

[142] Hopkins' poems were published by Oxford University Press, edited by Robert Bridges, in 1918. as *Poems of Gerard Manley Hopkins*. Quotations in this chapter are taken from the 5th impression with additional poems, edited by W.H. Gardner (Oxford University Press, 1956).

> I cannot in conscience spend time on poetry, neither have I the inducements and inspirations that make others compose. Feeling, love in particular, is the great moving power and spring of verse and the only person that I am in love with seldom, especially now, stirs my heart sensibly.

Presumably, 'the only person I am in love with' is God. In his *Letter* Coleridge had said he had lost the power of joy because he had lost human love. Because Hopkins was 'in love' with an imaginary divine being, who could not love him in return, he was deprived of the human warmth he so desperately needed. The 'terrible sonnets' he wrote at the end of his life are among the most searing poems of absence, lack and desolation ever written in English. Coleridge had been a 'metaphysical mountaineer' and Hopkins echoes him in his sonnet: 'No worst, there is none':

> O the mind, mind has mountains, cliffs of fall
> Frightful, sheer, no-man fathomed. Hold them cheap
> May who ne'er hung there.

He cries to God: 'Comforter, where, where is your comforting?' and receives no comfort. He is miserable in Dublin, a stranger, away from his family, friends and country. He still struggles not to despair (which is 'carrion comfort') but is thwarted:

> I am in Ireland now; now I am at a third
> Remove. Not but in all removes I can
> Kind love both give and get. Only what word
> Wisest my heart breeds dark heaven's baffling ban
> Bars or hell's spell thwarts.

The supernatural power to whom he has given his love and allegiance becomes a 'baffling ban', indistinguishable from 'hell's spell'. It has let him down totally and to make things worse, in orthodox terms (which this poem goes far beyond), it has got to be his fault. It leaves him 'a lonely began'.

His nights are dark indeed:

> I wake and feel the fell of dark, not day.
> What hours, O what black hours we have spent
> This night! What sights you, heart, saw; ways you went!
> And more must, in yet longer light's delay.
> With witness I speak this. But where I say
> Hours I mean years, mean life. And my lament
> Is cries countless, cries like the dead letters sent
> To dearest him that lives alas! away.

The poet, for whom 'self flashes off frame and face', experiences his own selfhood as pure negativity, as hell:

> Selfyeast of spirit a dull dough sours. I see
> The lost are like this, and their scourge to be
> As I am mine, their sweating selves; but worse.

In two following sonnets he prays for patience and resolves 'my own heart let me more have pity on'. But almost his last poem (written on March 17th 1889) is a meditation on a text from Jeremiah: 'Thou art indeed just, Lord if I contend/With thee' and asks: 'Why must/disappointment all I endeavour end?' Spring has come again but its joy does not reach him:

> ...See banks and brakes
> Now, leavèd how thick! lacèd they are again
> With fretty chervil, love and fresh wind shakes
> Them; birds build — but not I build; no, but strain,
> Time's eunuch, and not breed one work that wakes.
> Mine, O thou lord of life, send my roots rain.

There was no one to answer his prayer and he died on 8th June 1889. As with Coleridge, the power of joy was related to loving and being loved in return, which an imaginary supernatural figure did not do. The poem's image is of fatherhood: a dry impotence makes the poet unable to 'breed one work that wakes'. In his *Letter* Coleridge said of nature:

> O Sara! We receive but what we give,
> And in *our* life alone does Nature live.

This is even more true of an imaginary God. Nature is at least visible and Coleridge's *Letter* is partly a dialogue with Wordsworth's *Ode* about the interaction of the human mind with nature. God lives entirely 'in *our* life alone', because he is a human creation.

Following a long tradition, Hopkins' earlier, less desperate poems, describe his relationship to God — usually 'Christ our Lord' — as a love affair, in which he plays the feminine part. It has often been noted that the panting rhythm is orgasmic in the climax of the 'Wreck of the Deutschland', the moment of the nun's surrender to death and the poet's own surrender when 'I did say yes':

> But how shall I... make me room there:
> Reach me a... Fancy come faster—
> Strike you the sight of it? Look at it loom there,
> Thing that she... there then! the Master,
> *Ipse,* the only one, Christ, King, Head.

In the last four lines of the verse the 'bride' glories in her triumphant hero lover:

> He was to cure the extremity where he had cast her;
> Do, deal, lord it with living and dead;

> Let him ride, her pride, in his triumph, despatch and have
> done with his doom there.

Hopkins' ravishment with the beauty of nature often combines with his love affair with Christ. In 'Hurrahing in the Harvest':

> ...I walk, I lift up heart, eyes,
> Down all that glory in the heavens to glean our Saviour.

A little further on, the poem has the gorgeously erotic two lines, described by his editor, Robert Bridges, as an 'error of taste':

> And the azurous hung hills are his world-wielding shoulder
> Majestic — as a stallion stalwart, very-violet sweet!

Or in 'The Windhover' after the marvellous excitement of the bird's flight:

> ...the fire that breaks from thee then, a billion
> Times told lovelier, more dangerous, O my chevalier!

Unlike Wordsworth's 'something far more deeply interfused', in Hopkins' mystical moments of union with nature, the presence he feels is of an ideal hero lover, whom he addresses. His delight in 'mortal beauty' and his own sensuality is a spring of joy in him, which he regards as 'dangerous'. Fastening his feelings on Christ provides a permissible outlet for his sensuality, which in his best poems (such as 'Hurrahing in the Harvest' and 'The Windhover' quoted above) freely unites with the thrilling detail of natural beauty in a single dynamic moment of ecstasy. The moment, the poem, intertwines the 'double helix' of the erotic (albeit for an imaginary lover, nevertheless one in whom the poet still has confidence) and 'cosmic union' with nature in an experience of being abundantly, intensely alive, together with everything else that is. The poem *is* the ecstatic moment of intense life.

Some of Hopkins' other poems are marred by a split between the two halves of the sonnet form, expressing an irreconcilable conflict of feeling in a jarring change of tone. For example, the octet of 'Spring' expands in lovely synaesthetic images: 'thrush through the echoing timber does so rinse and wring/the ear' and 'the glassy peartree leaves and blooms, they brush/the descending blue'. But the sestet ruins the poem, wrenching it back in line with cheap religiosity. This conflict persisted throughout his career as a Jesuit and none of his major poems was published in his lifetime. In the circumstances, it is remarkable that he remained true to his own poetic inspiration and gave us his extraordinarily beautiful poems praising the thisness, 'inscape', 'instress' of nature and humanity. This will be explored further in Part 2 of this chapter, whose title comes, of course, from Hopkins: 'Self flashes off Frame and Face'.

John of the Cross[143] was born in 1542 and lived in Spain at a time when the Inquisition was savagely active and the Spanish crown was consolidating its genocidal empire in America. Philip II became King of Spain in 1556. The Council of Trent, which inaugurated the Counter-Reformation, closed in 1563. As well as violent political power struggles between the higher clergy, there was brutal infighting between the two branches of the Carmelite order — the 'calced' ('shod') and the stricter 'discalced' ('unshod' or barefoot) Carmelites, who included John. On December 2nd 1577 John was abducted from his convent in Avila by 'calced' monks, aided by the civil power, severely beaten up and imprisoned in the Toledo monastery in a tiny closet, which had been a lavatory and had only a slither of natural light. After six months of regular beatings and other ill-treatment, he was given

---

[143] Quotations from John of the Cross' poems are taken from *Obras de San Juan de la Cruz* (Editorial Apostolado de la Prensa, Madrid 1954). The translations are slightly revised versions from *García Lorca and John of the Cross*, translated by Dinah Livingstone (Katabasis, 1968).

writing materials and it was in this prison that he wrote most of his famous *Canticle*.

The *Canticle* is a dialogue between the Bride and Bridegroom in the tradition of the *Song of Songs*. The Bride does most of the talking. Her first line, which begins the poem, is: 'Where have you hidden yourself?' She chases him and in the end she gets him and the poem concludes with blissful union. The poem is an extraordinarily rich, beautiful and detailed expression of female sexuality through the process of falling in love, urgent chase to consummation — all the more extraordinary with its author being a celibate male. At the beginning of the poem she is wildly in love and he is not there. She asks the 'creatures' if he has passed their way. They give hints of him:

*Y déjame muriendo
un no sé qué que quedan balbuciendo.*

And what slays me
is I-don't-know-what that they keep stammering

He has stolen her heart:

*Y pues me le has robado
por qué así le dejaste
y no tomas el robo que robaste?*

Why did you take it
then leave it
and didn't want to keep what you had taken?

Messages are no good:

My love is an agony
which will not go away
unless it has your presence and your face.

She begs the crystal fountain to reflect:

The eyes for which I long
that are printed on the bottom of my soul.

The Bridegroom speaks to her for the first time, calling himself a 'stricken deer' — *she* is the huntress. (For John of the Cross, the divine beloved is much less macho than for Hopkins with that 'world-wielding shoulder'.) Bridegroom and Bride have a wonderful flowery baroque bed, 'draped in purple, built of peace and crowned with a thousand golden crowns'. There the Bride drinks in her beloved's 'inner wine cellar'.

Allí me dio su pecho,
allí me enseñó ciencia muy sabrosa
y yo le di de hecho
a mí sin dejar cosa,
allí le prometí de ser su esposa.

He gave me his heart
and sweet unimaginable knowledge
and I gave to him
everything I am.
There I promised him myself in marriage.

This is the betrothal (with no qualms at all about pre-marital sex). It is the beginning of intimacy, which increases. They will go up the mountain to its hidden caves, where they will drink 'pomegranate wine'.

Allí me mostrarías
aquello que mi alma pretendía
y luego me darías
allí tú, vida mía
aquello que me diste el otro día.

> There you would show me
> what my soul desires so urgently
> and then you would give me,
> you, my life, to me,
> what you gave me once the other day.

Throughout the poem the Bride is the protagonist. She is quite clear what she wants and she gets it. This in itself is subversive, even startling. It is an amazing poem, even if read purely as a human love poem. But that was not the author's intention; he wanted it read *'a lo divino'*, as an allegory of union with God. If we take it for granted that all gods are creations of the human Poetic Genius, can the poem still say anything to us?

We turn briefly to another love poem by John of the Cross, 'The Dark Night'. Again the woman is the protagonist, active and resourceful. Unobserved and in disguise, she slips out of the house to meet her lover on a dark night.

> *¡Oh Noche que guiaste!*
> *¡oh Noche amable más que el alborada!*
> *¡oh Noche que juntaste*
> *amado con amada*
> *amada en el amado transformada!*

> Oh Night that guided!
> Oh Night more delightful than the dawn!
> Oh Night that united
> beloved with beloved —
> her he loved transformed into beloved him!

Because English past participles are ungendered, the translation is more cluttered than the Spanish and cannot exactly reproduce the simplicity and sense of pairing and reciprocity of the two Spanish past participles (used as nouns), *amado* (= beloved, masculine) and *amada* (= beloved, feminine). Nevertheless the translation conveys the commingling, that she is *transformed* into him. Even the most ecstatic sexual union does not *transform* the woman into the man: they remain two people. It seems possible that, like other mystics, John is using this metaphor for subversive purposes (at a time when subversion was mortally dangerous). If the human being (the 'bride') is transformed into God (the 'bridegroom'), she *becomes* God, that is to say, human and God are indistinguishable. God is her life (*'tú, vida mía'*) but in the literal sense, her life is not separate from herself. It is not accidental that the metaphor's vehicle for this subversion is female sexuality, which the Church authorities had long regarded as anarchic, uncontrollable and untrustworthy. As Meister Eckhardt had put it centuries earlier:

> What is life? God's being is my life, but if it is so, then what is God's must be mine and what is mine God's. God's isness (*istikeit*) is my isness, and neither more nor less.

'Isness' attempts to express 'being in the present indicative', that is, 'being-doing' (= is), but in the abstract (= -ness). In another passage Eckhardt puts it:

> God must become me and I must become God, so entirely one that 'he' and 'I' become one 'is' and act in this 'isness' as one.

Isn't this saying that 'all gods reside in the human breast'? Without things that are, isness is nothing, an abstraction. But 'acting in this isness' does not result in solipsism, because 'isness' in the world is not confined to me. All that is shares in this 'isness' — both nature and other people. In his mystical poetry John uses the erotic as a metaphor for the deep sense of union with 'isness', achieved in contemplation. 'Isness' is one. But the metaphor adds the dimension of *we* ('*Gocémonos, Amado*': let us enjoy ourselves, my love). The sense of union with 'isness' turns

'I' into 'we' — the language is almost straining to say 'we is' — we being everything that is, myself included but not myself alone. The metaphor embraces the sense of self-lack of myself alone; the 'I' needs to become 'we' for its own survival. The metaphor also adds the dimension of profound love. All this can only be done in a poem that operates on several levels, making the poem itself the mystical experience. Writing in his horrible prison, John experienced the joy of creating the poem. Perhaps it saved his life.

Now we can compare the passage from Wordsworth's 'Tintern Abbey' quoted earlier with the Bride's ecstatic exclamation in the *Canticle*. Wordsworth felt:

>...a sense sublime
Of something far more deeply interfused,
Whose dwelling is the light of setting suns,
And the round ocean, and the living air,
And the blue sky, and in the mind of man...

The Bride exclaims:

>*Mi amado, las montañas*
los valles solitarios nemorosos
las ínsulas extrañas
los ríos sonorosos
el silbo de los aires amorosos.

>*La noche sosegada*
en par de los levantes del aurora
la música callada
la soledad sonora
la cena que recrea y enamora.

>My beloved is the mountains,
the solitary forests in the valleys,

the far-off islands
the sounding rivers
and the whisper of the loving breezes.

The tranquil night
and also the rising of the morning
music gone quiet,
solitude resonant,
the supper for refreshment and for love.

Both Wordsworth and John of the Cross have produced a list of beautiful things in nature, ending with something human. The main difference in the two passages is that the John of the Cross poem is a story, in which the list heightens the Bride's passion for her lover and the words are about him and addressed to him. The last line is the intimate 'supper for refreshment and for love'. In the Wordsworth passage the human is an autobiographical 'I', on the one hand, and the generalised 'mind of man' on the other. (However, later in the poem he turns to address his sister, Dorothy, who is really there with him and not a fiction.)

Coleridge had no hope of marrying Sara Hutchinson, but uses the word wedding several times in his *Letter* to her:

Joy, Sara! Is the Spirit and the Power
That wedding nature to us gives in Dower
A new Earth and a new Heaven.

He has lost this joy. The Bride in the *Canticle* is bursting with it and it transfigures the landscape for her *into* her lover, whom she is confident she *will* marry. At the end of the poem she says: 'Let us enjoy ourselves, my love.' Then: 'Let us go further into the thicket.'

In different ways, all four poets relate the power of joy — particularly joy in beauty and in love — to the power of poetry, both the power to create poetry and the power of the poetry created. (Paradoxically and unsustainably, sometimes their poetry is written out of the sense of loss of this joy, the sense of a joy-shaped void or shadow, the presence of its absence.) Poetry written out of 'the deep power of joy' not only describes the poet's own joy but communicates that joy to the reader, not as information but as illumination and as feeling. The power of joy springs from a sense of being intensely alive, a sense of sharing in the 'isness' of all that is. Poetry is its natural medium. Joy overflows. Joy demands expression and poetry is its articulating power.

'The *duende*,' said García Lorca at the beginning of the chapter, 'is a power and not a behaviour, it is a struggle and not a concept.' Its appearance is greeted with vociferous shouts of *Alá! Alá!*, 'God! God!' There is nothing supernatural about that. It is perfectly natural. The spirit and the power are a purely human quality, whose name is joy. Sweet joy befall thee!

2

SELF FLASHES OFF FRAME AND FACE

In Part 1 of this chapter we quoted the Dominican Eckhardt (1260-1328) on *isness*: 'God's isness (*istikeit*) is my isness, and neither more nor less.' Hopkins' favourite medieval philosopher, 'who of all men most sways my spirits to peace', was Eckhardt's near-contemporary, the Franciscan Duns Scotus (1266-1328). One of Scotus' ideas that most appealed to Hopkins was of *thisness* or, in Latin, *haecceitas*. For Scotus, thisness is the principle of individuation, that makes something or someone an individual.

Not long after first getting hold of Scotus' work, Hopkins wrote in his journal for July 19th 1872: 'Just then when I took in any inscape of the sky or sea I thought of Scotus.' Hopkins invented two terms with which to speak of thisness: instress and inscape. Instress (related to 'stress') can be regarded as the energy by which 'isness' keeps being realised or realising itself[145] within an individual to make it its active self. Inscape (related to 'landscape') is the thisness, the particularity, the selfhood of the individual, which 'flashes off frame and face'.

For Scotus, God is 'Being in itself', 'Being of itself', *ens per essentiam:* 'Being in its essence, Being of its essence'. For an atheist, this way of talking about being is an abstraction and God does not exist. But you do not have to believe in God to think of these two principles of 'isness' and 'thisness' as the twin fount of the poetry of Earth. 'Isness' is shared by everything that is and everyone who is, according to what and who they are. 'Isness' gives 'being' a more active emphasis. It is the life of living things, or as Hildegard of Bingen called it, referring both to nature and the human spirit, their 'greenness'. But as well as isness, each

---

[145] Rather like a Greek Middle Voice. See page 38.

individual thing or person has its — or his or her — own particular thisness or self. Poetry combines the praise and sense of pure being, which everything that is has in common, with that of the thisness, which anything that is has in particular.

Although 'God' is a poetic way of talking about 'isness' or 'being in itself', the more absolute this concept becomes, the less it makes sense to ascribe thisness to it. Another Scotus idea that appealed to Hopkins was that the Incarnation of Christ would have happened anyway, even if Adam had not sinned, because it was simply God's love that wanted the identification with humanity which the Incarnation involved. We can look on this as a prophetic way of saying that God would have become human anyway. Thisness belongs in our world, to the individual; it 'flashes off frame and face'. When the Word becomes incarnate, he is *this* individual. Thus Christ the Incarnate Word becomes the Poem of Humanity as well as the paradigm of poetry, which is also 'incarnate word', because a poem not only praises the combination of isness and thisness, but combines them in itself.

The 'Deutschland' sank in the mouth of the Thames on 7th December 1875. Hopkins' poem, 'The Wreck of the Deutschland' broke his seven-year-long poetic silence (except for 'two or three little presentation pieces') upon becoming a Jesuit. In the first, intensely personal, section, this is how he writes the centrality of the Incarnation:

> Not out of his bliss
> Springs the stress felt
> Nor first from heaven (and few know this)
> Swings the stroke dealt —
> Stroke and a stress that stars and storms deliver,
> That guilt is hushed by, hearts are flushed by and melt —
> But it rides time like riding a river
> (And here the faithful waver, the faithless fable and miss.)

> It dates from day
> Of his going in Galilee;
> Warm-laid grave of a womb-life grey;
> Manger, maiden's knee...

Incarnation requires a date, a place and a history. In chapter III we considered poetry and presence and the relation between the 'now' of eternity and the fleeting 'now' of time — presence as *here now*. The condition of being and living on Earth is that thisness realises isness through changing time and place — *this* here and now. Being and living *flow*. As Blake puts it in *The Marriage of Heaven and Hell*[146]: 'Energy is the only life and is from the Body and Reason is the outward bound or circumference of Energy. Energy is Eternal Delight.' But this does not mean, as some postmodernists have maintained, that the 'self' completely dissolves. Even with things, a tree for example, a poem may 'catch' *this* tree at *this* moment. But the winter tree is still itself when it puts out leaves in spring. Obviously, many philosophical problems arise, such as, is a seedling a tree? Nevertheless, clearly we can say a tree remains *itself* from January to December, even though it passes through seasons and grows.

Despite even tougher philosophical problems, this applies even more strongly to human beings with *consciousness*. The aim of torture is to destroy a human self and the strength with which some people have resisted this is almost incredible.

This section will take some examples of how poets have spoken about thisness and self, starting with Hopkins and his special terms, instress and inscape. His phrase 'self flashes off frame and face' suggests the distinction between things and people (who have faces) and we will look first at some examples of the

---

[146] Plate 4.

thisness of things and secondly, of people. Then we will turn to the human self as an *ongoing creation* through *self-expression* and consider poem-writing as a type of this. The persistent writing of poems throughout a lifetime can amount to a *body of work*. How might that relate to the self as a project? Finally, we consider the thisness of the poem itself, in its linguistic particularity, as incarnate word. This particularity accounts for the notorious difficulty of translating poetry, but it is not impossible because of what human beings and languages, despite their distinctness, have in common.

In his journal for April 8th 1873 Hopkins wrote:

> The ashtree growing in the corner of the garden was felled. It was lopped first: I heard the sound and looking out and seeing it maimed there came at that moment a great pang and I wished to die and not to see the inscapes of the world destroyed anymore.

In 1879, when he was back at Oxford he wrote 'Binsey Poplars'. The poem begins by conveying the inscape of the 'fresh and following folded rank' of the felled trees 'whose airy cages quelled/Quelled or quenched in leaves the leaping sun.' Their destruction is an 'unselving', both of each tree and the scene the group creates:

> ...only ten or twelve
> Stroke of havoc unselve
> The sweet especial scene.

At its beginning the poem *conjures up* the beautiful inscape of the trees and goes on to lament the *unselving*. This is the poem's strength. After the powerful, invented word 'unselve', the poem's last three lines, rather than conjuring up the scene, read more like a private *reference* to it, in the unoriginal style of a Victorian ditty:

161

The sweet especial scene
Rural scene, rural scene
Sweet especial rural scene.

This place was special to the poet and had special meaning for him. Like the trees which are its subject, in 'Binsey Poplars' the poem's own inscape is sustained up to the word 'unselve'. Then, like the trees, the poem itself collapses and is 'unselved'.

A modern poet and apple specialist, Michael Hamburger, has written many poems about trees. His book, *Trees* is a series of poems conveying the 'whatness' or *quidditas* of each species, the 'oakness' of oak, the 'birchness' of birch and so on. Here are just a few lines from 'Oak':[147]

Oak has an earthward urge, each bough dithers,
Now rising, now jerked aside, twisted back,
Only the bulk of the lower trunk keeps
A straight course, only the massed foliage together
Rounds a shape out of knots and zigzags.

The effect of the poem is to make you want to look at a particular oak tree and see how that tree *realises* the poem's description of oak, how *thisness* embodies *quiddity*. In Scotist terms, although we can speak of the essence (for example, of oak), the essence does not in fact exist without individuation as *this* oak tree.

Growing things survive through different seasons and all kinds of weather. The changeableness of the English weather has inspired much poetry: today the weather is like *this* and affects things like *this*. Hopkins' 'Hurrahing in the Harvest' exults in a particular sky, whose beauty is in motion and changing all the time:

---

[147] From Michael Hamburger, *Trees* (Ember Handpress, Llangynog 1998).

... up above, what wind-walks! What lovely behaviour
Of silk-sack clouds! Has wilder wilful-wavier
Meal-drift moulded ever and melted across skies?

'Pied Beauty' is his great hymn of praise for 'dappled things':

For skies of couple-colour as a brinded cow;
For rose-moles all in stipple upon trout that swim;
Fresh fire-coal chestnut-falls; finches' wings;
Landscape plotted and pieced — fold, fallow, and plough;
And all trades, their gear, tackle and trim.

Many poems focus on *this* place, *this* creature, *this* thing that has a special significance to the poet. To give just one modern example, Andrew Hawthorne's poem 'The Losing of Childhood'[148] describes a family climbing up a cliff path with hairpin bends. At each bend they pause to look back at how the glorious sandcastle, which the child spent all afternoon on the beach building, has been destroyed a bit more by the sea. The child bursts into tears and will not be comforted:

There will be other beaches, more castles,
we promised you. Grander, stronger,
more memorable.

But not this one again, you said,
not this one.

The appreciation of thisness involves feeling the pain of mortality, not just of *this* sandcastle but of *this* child.

---

[148] In Andrew Hawthorne, *Strange Music of Bone* (Katabasis, 1998)

In his poem 'To what Serves Mortal Beauty?' Hopkins, who was so sensitive to beauty, in things, trees, animals and people but who regarded it as 'dangerous', recommends:

Love what are love's worthiest, were all known;
World's loveliest — men's selves. Self flashes off frame and face.

One of his best known poems about a particular person is his sonnet 'Felix Randal', written in Liverpool in 1880. 'Felix Randal, the farrier' died of consumption. The poem describes how 'sickness broke him' and though 'he cursed at first' he eventually submitted to the ministrations of a priest (Hopkins). Unlike the sonnet 'Spring', in which I consider the octet to be superb and the sestet marred by religiosity, here it is the octet has touches of Victorian clericalism such as 'since I had our sweet reprieve and ransom/Tendered to him.'

Nevertheless, the octet graphically conveys the powerful blacksmith's physical collapse. And the sonnet form works well as a whole to give us the man. It has a beautiful turn, which starts to gather with the sestet's 'poor Felix Randal' (Felix was his Christian name but the surname Randal was invented to rhyme with 'sandal'), and breaks like a great wave in the splendid last three lines, recalling him in the days of his strength:

How far from then forethought of, all thy more boisterous years,
When thou at the random grim forge, powerful amidst peers,
Didst fettle for the great grey drayhorse his bright and battering
                                                                            sandal.

This conclusion conveys the magnificent energy of this blacksmith's working life, the life-energy he shared with 'the great grey drayhorse', whose horseshoes he 'fettled' with red-hot fire. In just three lines the poem conjures up a particular life in a picture charged with mythical resonance. The last line, in particular, uses mythic association, alliteration and assonance to fix the figure of Felix Randal in the reader's mind. Literally, the line is so beautiful and strong that it is hard to get it out of your head. It is Hopkins' homage to the power and dignity of this manual worker. As a priest, he attended this *same* man on his sickbed, until he died of consumption in a miserable slum. That is, it was the *same* man but he was not the *same*.

Here Hopkins' favourite theologian, Duns Scotus, is illuminating in his definition of the principle of individuation as *haecceitas*, thisness. Scotus rejected the neoplatonist idea that embodiment is a fall or descent for the individual soul, but he also debated against the then current Aristotelian doctrine that the principle of individuation is reducible to the particular chunk of matter that a body consists of. For him, individuation was *related* to the body, but he was not known as the 'Subtle Doctor' for nothing.

His term *haecceitas* tried to do justice to the complex way in which, for example, we can rightly say 'this man' of a man whose physical condition is so greatly changed. Even though every single cell in my body may be exchanged at some time during my life, I still call it 'my body' — one body with a history. The force and pathos of Hopkins' poem derives from the fact that this weak, dying consumptive to whom he ministered, was still Felix Randal, the man who once, 'powerful amidst peers' was blacksmith to the great drayhorses, who pulled enormous loads through the city of Liverpool. Thisness is related to the body because it is mortal. The poetry of Earth is the poetry of mortal being. It is *incarnate* word.

Felix Randal was not an intimate friend of Hopkins. He was one of his parishioners. Intimacy means coming close to the self of another, for example, a child, a lover, a friend. Intimacy means respecting the thisness of the other, both now as it 'flashes off frame and face' and as it develops through time. Simone de

Beauvoir says that maternal love 'does not imply reciprocity', meaning a mother's love should respect the child's thisness and development towards independence and not demand the same in return from her child before he or she is grown up. On the other hand, intimate love and friendship between adults does 'imply reciprocity', that is, mutual respect for the self of the other. Of course, all sorts of relationships occur in which that does not happen or happens unequally, or the 'self' of the other respected is not the 'self' as the other sees him or herself.

All this is the stuff of drama. Poetry catches the thisness of self 'flashing' out of the turbid medium of human relationships. In Shakespeare, for example, flawed heroes, such as Hamlet, brave, ambitious men who deteriorate into villains, such as Macbeth, or even hardened villains, such as Iago and Richard III, are all complex characters who are very strongly themselves. Human relationships vary along a scale from the most positive and loving to the most negative, where 'hell is other people', as in Sartre's *Huis Clos,* or the non-relationship, where 'Hell is oneself, Hell is alone, the other figures in it merely projections', as in Eliot's *The Cocktail Party.* As Hopkins expressed this in one of his 'terrible sonnets':

> ...I see
> The lost are like this, and their scourge to be
> As I am mine, their sweating selves; but worse.

On the other hand, the heightened awareness of being in love responds passionately to the *thisness* of the beloved, who is *this* person with *this* face, because, as the Bride says in the John of the Cross' *Canticle,* 'no one else will do'. Don't send another messenger, she pleads:

Descubre tu presencia
y máteme tu vista y hermosura;

mira que la dolencia
de amor que no se cura
sino con la presencia y la figura.

Give me your presence
and let me die of seeing you and your grace.
My love is an agony
that will not go away
unless it has your presence and your face.

Heaven and hell exist, not in an afterlife but 'in the human breast'. The dialectics of self/other are multiple — between self as hellish isolation and other as the longed-for beloved, as comfort and growth; between self/other in relationships, which are themselves *particular* in their innumerable positive and negative configurations.

Despite his personal experience of the self as hell, and despite all his religious fears and scruples about 'mortal beauty', Hopkins asserts *himself* in his deepest poetic insight:

Love what are love's worthiest, were all known;
World's loveliest — men's selves. Self flashes off frame and face.

This beauty 'does set dancing blood' and also 'keeps warm/Men's wits to the things that are; what good means.' Poetry *apprehends*, *captures* the 'flashing' self in 'O-seal-that-so feature', which so moves us. But the human self involves more than the fleeting moment of glimpsed beauty. The self apprehended in this transitory moment has a *history* of human living, of dealing with 'the things that are' and 'what good means'. Human mortality does not imply (as the postmodernist flirtation with 'the East' has suggested) that the human self is reducible to a series of passing moments, that the self has no persistence at all and we are just a series of selves.

Mortality means that human beings have a *lifespan*, of birth, growth, decay and death. Human beings *change* throughout their lifespan but that does not mean they cease to be themselves. I change but I can also adapt and apply to myself the reiterated 'same' of the great christological definition at Chalcedon,[149] I am the *self-same* one who was born at that particular time and place, who went to that school, have lived in this house since 1966. Felix Randal was a *changed man* when he lay dying on his sickbed, but he was still Felix Randal. The self *both* persists *and* changes, for better or worse.

The dramatic climax of Webster's *Duchess of Malfi* is the moment when the false servant Bosola, who has agreed with her brothers to have her strangled, enters her prison and she asks him: 'Who am I?' Bosola says:

> Thou art a box of worm-seed, at best but a salvatory of green mummy. What's this flesh? A little crudded milk, fantastical puff-paste. Our bodies are weaker than those prisons boys use to keep flies in; more contemptible, ours is to preserve earthworms.

'I am Duchess of Malfi still!' She proclaims with her whole self that she is still herself, even if she no longer has anything that belongs to a duchess and knows she is about to die.

The dissolution of the self into a series of fleeting momentary selves is deeply anti-humanist and trivialises the project of any individual human life and the collective struggle of any human group. The human self is infinitely more interesting than a series of 'dancing atoms' that occasionally give us a buzz. The thisness of a human self is not just the fleeting moment of 'O-seal-that-so

---

[149] Quoted on pages 113-114.

feature' but the historical human person whose feature it is, who is not individuated merely by the changing atoms of his or her physical makeup, but by a *haecceitas* — thisness — that is related to *this* body, that persists, despite physical changes, throughout a lifespan. The self that flashes off frame and face in a moment of startling beauty is not reducible to that moment of revelation.

In that fleeting epiphanous moment, poetry apprehends the thisness of the self, both in this instance of its beauty and in its human history. The poetry is in the humanity, which embraces both the particular moment of beauty, and all that goes to make *this* mortal and linguistic self throughout a lifetime. Failure, waste and mortality touch us more because of the potential glory of 'the human form divine'. The poetry is in the pity but also in the glory. John the Evangelist says of the divine incarnate Word: 'We have seen his glory.' What flashes off the human frame and face is the speaking self.

Here are just two examples from contemporary poems. First, this is the beginning of Jane Kirwan's poem 'Coursework'.[150] The speaker is the mother of a teenage daughter, in whom the *inscape* of the once small girl persists in the difficult adolescent she has grown into 'in the curve of her neck' and 'swell of a back/that is more like her father's.' The mother has lost her little girl, can only feel anxious about the earlobe infection, which her teenager, thrusting for autonomy, is 'dealing with herself'. For the mother, helping her daughter wash her hair 'remains one thing that I can do'.

She apprehends, in *this* inscape of neck and back, the *self* of her daughter — kneeling by the bath — with a history going back to conception, when the father passed on his features, through the enormous changes from childhood to the brink of adulthood.

---

[150] In Jane Kirwan, *Stealing the Eiffel Tower* (Rockingham Press, Ware 1997).

The unexpected first line, the stronger for being all monosyllables except for the pivotal 'again', conveys this shock of acknowledgment:

> I know her again in the curve of her neck,
> rinse conditioner through knotted hair
> as she kneels by the bath
> silent for a moment
>
> reprieve from sulks about empty freezers
> doors slamming at dawn, black lipstick.
> The infection in the fourth hole of her ear lobe
> she is dealing with herself.
>
> I massage her scalp.
> This remains one thing that I can do.
> Smell of almond, swell of a back
> that is more like her father's.

The second example is the first verse and concluding verses of Anne Beresford's 'Dichotomy',[151] dedicated to her friend Eva Hoffmann. The final quatrain describes the 'dichotomy' between a life that has witnessed both a 'world of human horror' and 'a perfection beyond words', as 'almost a miracle'. The miracle is the self that has *survived* the human horror and *persists* in the deep pleasure of this friendship. The poet apprehends this self from her friend's *face*, the tranquillity that flashes or perhaps beams off it, so that 'ordinary day to day activities/become illuminated.' The dichotomy is not a *succession* of selves, but two halves of an *integral* self, 'participant' in both hell and heaven, whose face and whose presence tranquilly *shine,* as *this* single, ordinary, miraculously whole, human being.

---

[151] In Anne Beresford, *No Place for Cowards* (Katabasis, 1998).

Perhaps it is the darkness
the division of the soul
or the confusion of aloneness
in a place teeming with life...

In your face — tranquillity
in your presence
ordinary day to day activities
become illuminated

Shopping with you in a supermarket
supper on the balcony, candles lit
to keep away mosquitoes,
moments which have become important in my mind
struggling to reach an understanding

To be a participant
in a world of human horror
and a perfection beyond words
is almost a miracle

It has been said that our own time has witnessed a greater drive for individuation, to 'be myself' or 'do my own thing', than any previous age. Whether or not this is the case, it is commonly assumed today that the way to 'be myself' is through 'self-development', and the way to 'do my own thing' is through 'self-expression'. If we are lucky we may get a job that pays us to do these things. However, few people have a job which enables them to become everything they want to be; many jobs are unfulfilling, even dehumanising, and some people have no job at all. Although they still need to get a living elsewhere, people may turn to the arts for self-development and expression, both as consumers and producers. Quite a large number turn to poetry. Nevertheless, the proliferation of poetry workshops does not, of course, mean that more good poetry is being written than in the past.

One criterion of good poetry is how much of themselves people put into writing poems. For those who, with greater or lesser success, put all of themselves, or what matters most to them of themselves, into their poems, their poetry becomes their speaking self. If self is both *thisness* and *becoming,* one way in which it becomes is by *accumulating* experiences, memories, resonances, etc. In the case of those who put themselves into writing poetry, as well as accumulating experiences, they accumulate a *body of work,* which is their self-expression both of themselves as an individual, and in relation to other people and the world.

Individual self-expression says: 'Here I am.' Self-expression in relation to others covers the broad scope from intimate personal relationships to political witness: 'Here I stand.' Self-expression does not have to be *confessional.* The self-expression can be in the *work* of producing poems and one mark of mature poets is that they are interested in *other people,* as well as themselves. A poet's body of work can be described as *self becoming word* and a touchstone for judging this body of work is its *coherence.*

As well as a body of work being a kind of body, so is each single poem. A poem is a form of incarnation or embodiment, in which thoughts and images, shaped in particular words in a particular language, are *articulated* by putting these words together in a particular way and order to form a whole hearable (or readable) entity, which must 'come alive'. The form of the poem may be traditional, such as a sonnet. Whether the sonnet comes alive will depend on *this* articulation of these particular words. Hopkins often used the sonnet form (including 'curtal' sonnets), adapted for his purposes. The sonnet 'Felix Randal' is rhymed: *abba abba ccd ccd.* It is written in 'sprung rhythm' with six stresses per line. As we saw in the discussion of this poem, and of 'Spring' earlier,[152] sometimes the two halves of the sonnet express the two 'sides' — the priest and the poet — of Hopkins himself.

Today much poetry is 'free verse'. Poets 'do their own thing' or perhaps twentieth century poets have felt the need for free verse to say fresh things, for which they considered the old forms tired or worn out. But just as 'self-expression' can degenerate into self-indulgence, 'free verse' may fail to emerge from wordy prosing and remain *tohu* and *bohu* — 'formless and empty' — like the primal chaos in Genesis before 'Let there be light'. As well as creating the poem, the free-verse poet has to create the form to fit it. The poem needs frame and face, off which its *self* can flash.

The contemporary free-verse poet can draw on a long tradition and all the prosodic resources of the language. We have looked briefly at some of these resources in earlier chapters and there is no space here to discuss them in more detail. Countless examples spring to mind of the ways in which free verse poems have adapted or created a form to suit themselves, written not only in English, but in all the many other languages in which poetry is produced. We could also quote countless translations.

This book has already noted the notorious difficulty of translating poetry and given various examples. Because it is so difficult it therefore remains an irresistible challenge. Perhaps we could adapt Tertullian's famous phrase and say 'we do it because it is impossible'. But translation is also a vital way of enabling readers to expand their reading beyond their own language and tradition. Reading in the original language is best but translation is better than nothing.

As this section is concerned with 'self', it is also fascinating to consider the 'self' of a translation. If a translation succeeds as a

---

[152] 'Felix Randal' on pages 164-5; 'Spring' in Part 1 of this chapter on page 150.

poem in the new language, then it will have its own 'self' but if the translation is faithful, this self must remain closely related to the original. We have all had the experience of seeing someone in the street, who from a distance looks just like someone we know, but closer up we see that this person, though physically very similar, is a different person, maybe from a completely different background. Perhaps we could compare a poem and its translation to identical twins brought up in different cultures. Such comparisons, of course, only give an inkling of the translator's task.

As the poetry of Earth is superabundant, we could continue indefinitely. For now we finish with just one example of the *thisness* of a poem itself, written in English, and borrow the disclaimer that concludes John's gospel: 'Were every one of them to be written, I suppose that the world itself could not contain the books that would be written.'

Here is Kathleen McPhilemy's 'Blackthorn',[153] set in the Oxfordshire countryside in the 1990s:

Who has seen the blackthorn
gift of the lengthening evenings?
Pledging another spring
it mantles the edge of the wood
and white as the ghost of March
flowers by the edge of the road.

Whose is the blackthorn blossom?
Does it belong to the name at Lloyds
who owns these woods and fields?
Where among the shivering walls
that have built the cardboard city

---

[153] In Kathleen McPhilemy, *A Tented Peace* (Katabasis, 1995).

could the blackthorn blossom flower?

The flower itself is a wall
hiding that shameful city;
its fires of invisible anguish
are a white and burning bush.

The sprung rhythm three-beat line throughout gives the poem its urgent pace, despite the variation in line-length. It has two six-line verses (each starting with a question) and a concluding quatrain, which tightly structure its thought-process. There is no regular rhyme scheme, which could make it too neat, but the poem has its own peculiar music, appropriately using alliterative energy, with internal and various kinds of near-rhyme to strengthen its phonic coherence.

The first verse is the quietest in tone. The initial two-line question introduces 'the blackthorn/gift of the lengthening evenings' and softly raises expectations. Like the blackthorn, the poem itself appears to be 'pledging another spring'. 'Pledging another spring' is the first line of verse 1's concluding quatrain, which is held together by the internal rhyme 'pledging — edge — March — edge — (consonant rhyme, with voiced-voiceless affricate pairs: /dʒ/ as in edge, and /tʃ/ as in March) and the final consonant rhyme of lines 4 and 6: wood — road. The only uncomfortable hint is 'the ghost of March'.

The tone changes sharply with the question introducing the second six-line verse: 'Whose is the blackthorn blossom?' In this verse, instead of a quatrain interwoven with internal and near rhymes, we get two more questions, with the alliteration gathering force (**belong** underlining **blackthorn blossom**). 'Does it belong to the name at Lloyds/who owns these woods and fields?' Not quite a near-rhyme, 'fields' is a phonic echo of 'Lloyds'. The **b** alliteration is carried through in the third question of this second verse, 'flower' picks up 'fields', 'cardboard' alliterates with 'could' and the 'b' of its second syllable picks up the main 'b' alliteration of the whole verse: 'Where among the shivering walls/that have built the cardboard city/could the blackthorn blossom flower?' The alliterative energy becomes indignation.

Though each line still has three stresses, the final four-line verse has fewer unstressed syllables between stresses. Thus although the time between stresses is the same, there is less hurrying over unstressed syllables between them. This makes the rhythm tread more firmly, giving a riddle-solving, oracular authority to this concluding statement, which does not directly, but *does* indirectly, answer the preceding questions. The starkness of the statement is increased — not by a final full-rhyming couplet, which might sound too pat — but by a final couplet with an unstressed consonant rhyme: anguish/bush. The 'f' alliteration, which began in the preceding verse, becomes stronger — flower — shameful — fires — and we could add the 'v', which is the (labio-dental fricative) voiced pair to 'f', of: invisible. The last two words of the poem pick up the 'b' alliteration with 'burning bush'. Like this 'b' alliteration, the word 'white' (itself alliterating with 'wall') recapitulates the first verse description of the blackthorn blossom, which adds force and finality to the poem's end:

The flower itself is a **wall**
hiding that shameful city;
its **f**ires of invisible anguish
are a **w**hite and **b**urning **b**ush.

These are just some of the devices that make the poem *itself*. Its form draws on tradition and adapts it to suit itself and give shape to *these* words in *this* poem. This particular form shaping these particular words speaks; the poem is an articulate body of words. This well-shaped body has a self — the poem itself — which we can call incarnate word. As we said earlier, incarnation requires a date, a place and a history. This poem's language is English, it is set in Oxfordshire in the 1990s.

The country is ravishingly beautiful when the blackthorn blossoms in March but there is an *uneasiness* in the home counties and the poem raises questions. The beauty is also property, a commodity of the rich. In the second verse the pivot of the questions is the City and its shadow — the name at Lloyds (who is nameless) representing the wealth of capitalism that has built the 'shivering walls' of the 'cardboard city'. Deftly the poem takes the reader from the comforting expectations of a spring poem in the first line, to its startling conclusion:

> The flower itself is a wall
> hiding that shameful city.

The pain that created the wealth to buy the lovely spring hedges of Oxfordshire is well hidden. Then with another startling image, the poem's last two lines see the blackthorn *blazing* with blossom. The wall becomes a wall of fire: 'fires of invisible anguish'. The image leaps to the 'burning bush', seen by Moses.[154]

When God appears to Moses in the burning bush to order him to lead the people of Israel out of slavery in Egypt, Moses asks: 'If I come to the people of Israel and say to them, "The God of your fathers has sent me to you" and they ask, "What is his name?" what shall I say to them?' God replies to Moses: 'I AM WHO I AM.'

Earlier we quoted Hopkins' answer in his poem to the question in the poem's title, 'To what serves Mortal Beauty?' Hopkins' answer was:

---

[154] Exodus 3:1-15.

> ... See: it does this: keeps warm
> Men's wits to the things that are; what good means —

In Kathleen McPhilemy's poem 'Blackthorn' the blossom's 'mortal beauty' does precisely that. As a burning bush saying 'I AM', it keeps our wits alive 'to the things that are; what good means', which, in turn, averts us to what good does *not* mean. It bears witness as it blazes with beauty that kindles both love and rage. Or rather, it is evidence and epiphany whose witness is the poem itself.

Hopkins' poem on Mortal Beauty deals with his private anxieties as a celibate Jesuit. The 'professional religious' tone of the last three lines may jar on the secular reader. However, we can also read these lines as a warning not to commodify the beauty of the Earth and use it just for trading in order to accumulate so much property that it robs others of basic necessities. Of course, we need the means to live decently; of course we feel anxiety because our hard-earned wages, life's savings and old age pension are all implicated in the present money system and naturally we do not want to be poverty-stricken. But this is the answer Hopkins gives to his own anxious questioning:

> What do then? how meet beauty? Merely meet it; own,
> Home at heart, heaven's sweet gift; then leave, let that alone.

What do then? Do not appropriate the Earth in a way that deprives other people, much less in a way that destroys 'the inscapes of the world', including 'love's worthiest, were all known;/World's loveliest — men's selves.' Merely meet it. Self flashes off frame and face. The poetry of Earth is a common treasury, to be enjoyed, not because it is my commodity, but for itself.

CHAPTER VI
MORTAL BEAUTY

Planet Earth is our home and this essay has tried to distinguish the poetic qualities of its life: abundance, diversity, particularity and gratuitousness; time and mortality; 'thisness' containing and shaping 'isness'. It has looked at these qualities both in Earth's many life forms and in human cultures, with their many languages, religions and poetries — the different ways in which human beings make their home on Earth. We looked at how capitalism threatens this abundance and diversity, because for capitalism anything and everything can be treated as a commodity.

We reflected on poetry and presence, how the fleeting present moment of a poem can contain a whole past history and 'see' a future. In their many different languages, many human cultures write this poetry. Poetry is the heart of language and speaking human beings are the voice of the planet. Like a dawn chorus, this hugely diverse and abundant poetry has common qualities, which both express and embody the life on Earth it writes.

When a poem is a conversation in a particular cultural tradition, as well as recapitulating that past, it can look to the future. Abelard's hymn *O quanta qualia* looks forward eagerly to the joys of the heavenly Jerusalem. Atheists know that there is no heaven apart from what we can create ourselves on Earth, but that does not prevent a yearning for human fulfilment. Because poetry both praises and partakes of earthly life's abundance and diversity, the present moment of eternity in mortal time, the 'thisness of isness' and for-its-own-sakeness, it has a *utopic* quality itself. It offers a 'foretaste of utopia'. Its looking backwards to Eden is *prefigurative*.

As heaven can only be on Earth, we have to be prepared for the fact that it might never come. But part of poetry's pathos is that immortal longings are aroused by the beauty of mortal life.

In his hymn about the heavenly Jerusalem, Abelard speaks of the songs sung in heaven:

*Nec ineffabiles
cessabunt jubili
quos decantibimus
et nos et angeli.*

There'll be no ending
the unutterable praises
we and the angels
together shall sing.

The operative word is 'unutterable'. Angels have no bodies and are not in time. The bodiless cannot utter the songs and poems which are the poetry of Earth. Rhythmical human bodies, that live *and die* in time, in all their physical and linguistic abundance and diversity, in the thisness of their selfhood, sharing these qualities with the rest of life on Earth, are necessary to utter the poetry of Earth and give it its poignancy and power over other earthlings. *Mortal beauty* is the paradoxical stuff of this poetry. It has a utopic quality because it keeps our wits *warm*.

In chapter V we looked at two great *Odes* by Wordsworth and Coleridge as a poetic conversation on the dialectic between Earth's 'forms of beauty' and the 'shaping spirit of the Imagination'. Like Wordsworth, Mary Wollstonecraft was in France shortly after the French Revolution and had a love affair that was rapturous at its dawn. Daughter of the Enlightenment though she was, she wrote to her lover, Gilbert Imlay:

Imagination is the true fire, stolen from heaven, to animate this cold creature of clay — producing all those fine sympathies that lead to rapture, rendering men social by expanding their hearts.[155]

Of course, beauty and imagination do not automatically lead to justice, but they do create a longing for things to be 'just right', which *is* related — albeit not always directly — to an ache for justice. On the other hand, people were outraged by the counterfeit of this: Thatcher hiding the war-wounded so as not to spoil the 'beauty' of her victory parade. Possibly, the naivety of the 1960s was to assume the connection between beauty and justice *was* automatic: that 'flower power' inevitably led to 'love and peace', that *Imagination au pouvoir* automatically created a fair society. This was much too easy and certainly proved no bulwark against the unforeseen social vandalism of Thatcherism to come.

A medieval definition of beauty was *splendor formae*, the 'shining of shape', which also applies to a beautiful poem. As we saw in the theology of the Trinity, it was the Second Person, the Word who became incarnate, whose 'glory', John says, 'we have seen.' In the Trinity, Word flows into Love, Spirit (the Third Person), or to use Augustine's metaphor in 'my love is my weight', *gravitates* into it. Although, obviously in human beings, Word even in its most glorious poetic 'shining of shape' does not inevitably flow or gravitate into Love, Spirit, when poetic beauty warms us, we feel it is 'just right' that it should.

Augustine speaks of Beauty as 'so old and so new'. This is true of the Earth's beauty, Earth's poetry, which keeps bursting out in new life. It is also true of written poetry, which needs to seek new forms in order to keep bubbling up afresh. It is impossible for poetry to 'go back' to some golden age and just imitate it. That

---

[155] Quoted in Richard Holmes, *Footsteps* (Penguin, 1985).

would not be poetry but pastiche. Likewise, it is impossible for humanity simply to 'go back to nature'.

The original Eden is a dream with poetic and prefigurative power. It is a dream because humanity never was in a 'pure' state of nature; once humanity became human it was always 'cultural' as well as 'natural'. It is a dream because we know that life for early humans was 'nasty, brutish and short' and some taming of nature was essential for survival. We note that the Eden image of paradise is not a jungle but a *garden*.[156] It is a dream because there is no way in which the number of human beings now alive could be sustained by hunting and gathering or even early agriculture. We need to treat the abundance and diversity of life on Earth with the utmost respect, but nevertheless a 'natural balance' on the human scale can only be justice. This has not yet been achieved on Earth, so it can only be a future to be struggled for, rather than a past womb, into which an adult human being can no longer fit.

However, just as poetry needs to keep finding new forms, so does the struggle for justice. In recent years there has been a growing alliance between 'greens' who are concerned with the damage being done to the Earth's environment and those who oppose global capitalism, because it threatens both the Earth's environment and denies a decent life to most of Earth's people. In chapter I, for example, we saw the Zapatistas trying to create new forms of struggle, which would advance on the traditional guerrilla tactics of the Latin American left. We saw the use made by their leader Marcos of the internet and looked at communiqués he had posted on it.

---

[156] And, as we saw on page 76, in William Morris' utopian novel, *News from Nowhere*, the future London becomes a *garden city* .

Of course, it cannot be the role of poetry to develop the best political tactics in the struggle for global justice. The left in England has been nervous of poetry, just as it is only relatively recently that it has become more aware of green issues. Nevertheless, the struggle for justice cannot be divorced from the struggle to preserve the poetry of Earth: to defend our endangered planet and humanity, 'world's loveliest — men's selves.' If we see Planet Earth as a single body, with common qualities pervading all its incredible poetry, then we will see the commitment to its survival as a single endeavour, which can only be a project of justice. Utopia can be nowhere but on Earth, because there is nowhere else for it to be; an ideal perfection is unattainable. Perfection is not required; only the best that we can do, which is certainly not being done at the moment. As the poet Eduardo Galeano puts it, what is vital is *caminando:* not to abandon the journey.

Now the depredations of global capitalism have upped the stakes. We not only suffer the pain of mortality, which is the common lot of life on Earth, but whose consolation is life's power to reproduce itself. We are outraged that so many of Earth's life forms and human cultures are being damaged, prematurely killed off or extinguished forever by the wanton destructiveness of greed for profit at all costs. The Earth herself is in danger.

Though it is not for poetry to dictate political action, neither is it true that poetry is separate from politics. It is distinct but not separate, because the poetry of Earth (both what we create and what perceive, each in its own way) *does* keep warm our wits, *does* render us social by expanding our hearts. As it constantly bursts out afresh, so old and so new, in all its abundance and diversity, its isness-in-thisness, it is the irrepressible, multifarious, ever-present witness to 'the things that are; what good means', which makes the conviction that life on Earth *matters* self-evident.

As the Chilean poet, Roberto Rivera-Reyes, insists in the title and last line of his poem for the Mapuches, who fought back against the conquistadors for hundreds of years from their home in great forests of 'hyperbolical oaks, monkey puzzles and noble pines': 'The Earth must stay free forever.'[157]

---

[157] 'The Earth Must Stay Free Forever', translated by Dinah Livingstone, is in Roberto Rivera-Reyes, *Dawn Hunters and other Poems* (Latin American Writers, London 1989).